Anthropology of Contemporary Issues

A SERIES EDITED BY
ROGER SANJEK

The Varieties of Ethnic Experience: Kinship, Class, and Gender among California Italian-Americans
BY MICAELA DI LEONARDO

American Odyssey: Haitians in New York City
BY MICHEL S. LAGUERRE

American Odyssey

HAITIANS IN NEW YORK CITY

Michel S. Laguerre

Cornell University Press

Ithaca and London

First published 1984 by Cornell University Press.
Published in the United Kingdom by
Cornell University Press Ltd., London.

International Standard Book Number (cloth) 0-8014-1685-X
International Standard Book Number (paper) 0-8014-9270-X
Library of Congress Catalog Card Number 83-21078
Printed in the United States of America
Librarians: Library of Congress cataloging information appears on the last page of the book.

The paper in this book is acid-free and meets the guidelines for permanence and durability of the Committee on Production Guidelines for Book Longevity of the Council on Library Resources.

For Betsie, Mytho, and Babby

Contents

MAPS

Preface

The massive emigration of Caribbean people to the United States is a phenomenon of recent origin; it was only after World War II that the presence of Caribbean immigrants began to be felt. Although Puerto Rican, Cuban, Haitian, Dominican, Jamaican, and Trinidadian immigrants have now become part of the social landscape of many American cities, very few studies have been carried out to unveil the process of their integration in American society; consequently the size of the West Indian population in the United States is not known with any precision.

American Odyssey focuses on the plight of Haitian immigrants, the latest wave of Caribbean immigrants—with the Cubans—to settle in large numbers in Miami and New York City. Despite the publicity they received as "boat people" during the spring of 1980, little is known about the socioeconomic adaptation of these people. Their voices have been unheard because of their triple minority status as black, foreign, and French- and Creole-speaking.

In the past few years, the mass media have periodically reported on U.S. policy toward Haitian refugees. Many mainstream political practitioners have turned deaf ears to the issue, however, because the U.S. government has continued its support of Jean-Claude "Baby Doc" Duvalier, Haiti's president for life, and because Haitian immigrants do not yet constitute a significant voting bloc. The black boat people fleeing an autocratic regime have been consistently denied the status of political refugees in the United States.

Charges that the U.S. government has discriminated against

Haitian refugees in their quest for political asylum have been made and substantiated. In a letter published in the *New York Times*, on August 23, 1973, Representatives Bella Abzug and Charles Rangel, Bishop Paul Moore, and seven others urged "all U.S. citizens to protest denial of asylum for Haitian exiles, some of them escaped political prisoners." The popular press, however, has continued to provide a negative and often inaccurate image of the Haitian immigrants. On July 23, 1975, for example, the *New York Times* portrayed them as refugees with "endemic problems of lack of education, unemployment, inability to speak English, being foreigners to U.S. blacks and being in the U.S. illegally." This portrayal by and large reflected the American public's general perception of Haitian immigrants.

Because Haitian immigrants are officially considered to be economic rather than political refugees, the majority have been denied political asylum. The State Department, according to the *Times* of October 17, 1976, maintained that "relaxation of rules could produce a flood of economic refugees from all over the Caribbean where governments have serious socioeconomic and political problems." The *Times* of November 6, 1976, however, asked "whether the U.S. is acting in accordance with U.N. Protocol relating to status of refugees ratified by the Senate in 1968," and reported that the governing board of the National Council of Churches had raised the question of "whether color is a factor."

The trips to Florida in leaking sailboats have taken their toll of Haitian lives. On July 23, 1978, the *New York Times* reported that a "boat carrying 28 Haitian refugees heading for Florida is hit by a storm and capsizes; unofficial figures show 10 refugees drowned, 3 are missing and 15 survived." One year later, on August 14, 1979, the *Times* reported that "5 children and 1 adult drowned after being pushed overboard by men allegedly paid to help them enter Florida illegally from Haiti; 10 others survived and 2 are missing." It further reported on January 21, 1980, that a "Haitian woman whose body washed ashore near the beach of a state park in Broward county, Florida, died after being shoved into the ocean by smugglers."

Contradictions in U.S. policies regarding Caribbean migrants were highlighted in the spring of 1980, when boatloads of Haitians and Cubans began to arrive in large numbers at the same Florida port at the same time. Many Americans thought that the U.S. government should admit the black Haitian immigrants as refugees for humanitarian if not for political reasons. U.S. Roman Catholic bishops issued a statement, published in the *New York Times* of May 2, calling for "immediate political asylum and permanent resident status for Haitian immigrants seeking safety in Florida." Other such appeals were made during May 1980 by Senator Edward Kennedy, the Congressional Black Caucus, the United Conference of Mayors, the Executive Council of the AFL-CIO, and the Council on Hemispheric Affairs. All of them compared the Haitian case with that of the Cubans and alleged that the U.S. government was discriminating against the black Haitians. According to the *Times* of May 6, for example, the Council on Hemispheric Affairs charged that the "U.S. allows Cubans political asylum almost without delay or question but is withholding the same designation from Haitians, who have fled political repression in their country."

On July 30, 1981, the U.S. government announced the experimental practice of holding Haitian refugees in detention camps, though this practice had been in force since May 20 (Mayers 1982:11). From the spring of 1981 to the summer of 1982, the practice was widely publicized and vigorously implemented. During this period the refugees were routinely sent to "jail-like conditions" or "concentration camps," *Newsweek* reported on February 1, 1982. During January 1982 there were "2,177 Haitians . . . in detention in the United States, at seventeen locations from subarctic New York state to sunny Puerto Rico." One month later, on February 28, the *Times* reported that 2,850 Haitians were "being held in U.S. detention centers or prisons in various states."

Two major events have helped to highlight the situation of the Haitian boat people in the detention camps. The *New York Times* reported on September 30, 1981: "President Reagan, in an apparent attempt to stem the flow of Haitian refugees into the U.S., issued an Executive Order authorizing the coast guard to intercept and turn around ships on the high seas that are suspected of carrying illegal immigrants." A few days later, "on October 11, 1981, the coast guard cutter *Hamilton*, on the order of the President of the United States, began its first full day of patrolling the Windward Passage between Haiti and Cuba" (Walsh 1981:335). And during the winter of 1982, the Reverend Jesse Jackson's trip to the Vatican to discuss with the pope the plight of Haitian refugees in the United States was well publicized. In his various television appearances, the charismatic leader of PUSH (People United to Save Humanity) has compared the situation of the recently arrived Polish immigrants who were granted political asylum with that of the Haitian boat people in the detention centers.

As a result of the wide publicity given the Krome Avenue Detention Center in Florida and Fort Allen in Puerto Rico, the camps were becoming an embarrassment to the U.S. government. During the Christmas season of 1981, the detainees at Krome staged a hunger strike. Outside the detention center sympathetic demonstrators, including representatives of the NAACP and the Union of American Hebrew Congregations, led by the Director of the Haitian Refugee Center, the energetic Reverend Gérard Jean-Juste, shouted angrily and in unison, "Asylum, yes! Deportation, no!" The television coverage of this well-attended nonviolent protest helped a great deal to publicize the Christmas message of the refugees to the rest of the nation. On April 28, 1982, the *Times* reported that women detainees had organized a hunger strike "to protest their incarceration at the refugee camp in Miami, Florida." The next month a special report concerning breast enlargement in Haitian males detained at Fort Allen was issued by the Inter-Regional Council for Haitian Refugees and sent immediately to the United Nations High Commission for Refugees, the Human Rights Commission in Geneva, and the Inter-American Commission for Human Rights of the Organization of American States in Washington, D.C.

Some of the detainees committed or attempted to commit suicide. Haitian refugee Yves H. Chapoteau, being held for deportation, was "found dead at Alden Correctional Facility in Buffalo, New York," according to the *Times* of December 4, 1981. The *Washington Post* reported on June 11, 1982, that according to a spokesperson for the Immigration and Naturalization Service (INS), "18 to 20 of the detainees have tried to commit suicide in the last two months."

While U.S. policy toward Haitian refugees was being criticized by progressive civic and religious organizations, the courts found it unacceptable on legal grounds. On July 3, 1980, the *New York*

Times reported that "U.S. Federal District Judge James L. King declares that the Immigration and Naturalization Service knowingly violated constitutional, statutory, treaty and administrative rights of thousands of Haitian refugees seeking political asylum in the U.S." Two other court decisions also found the government's detention practices illegal and ill advised. On March 5, 1982, Judge Robert L. Carter found "the detention of 53 Haitians in Brooklyn abusive and discriminatory" (Mayers 1982:11). On June 29, 1982, Judge Eugene P. Spellman ruled that the government practice of incarcerating Haitians "while they litigate their claims for admission to this country" was done "in a procedurally improper way" (Spellman 1982:41), and ordered the release of all Haitians then being held, with the exception of the fifty-three in Brooklyn, whose case was being tried separately (Mayers 1982:12).

The presence of Haitian detainees at the Krome Avenue Detention Center was considered by many leading politicians, including Governor Robert Graham and the Florida business community, to be a "moral disgrace" (Spellman 1982:1), and the state of Florida filed suit against the INS to have the camp shut down. The situation was no better at the detention camp in Puerto Rico. On July 26, 1982, a month after Judge Spellman ordered the release of Haitian detainees, *Time* reported that "at Fort Allen in Puerto Rico, 707 Haitians were forced to live in tents in sweltering 90° heat and rain, even though several unused buildings on the base offered better shelter."

As if to add fuel to the fire of protest over Haitian refugees, shortly after a three-judge panel of the Court of Appeals for the Eleventh Circuit in Atlanta upheld Spellman's decision to release 1,800 Haitian detainees from 14 detention camps, the popular media were rife with reports of the spread of a deadly new disease, acquired immunodeficiency syndrome (AIDS), among homosexuals, intravenous drug abusers, hemophiliacs, and Haitian refugees. Recent reports from the Centers for Disease Control in Atlanta have also helped to make cases of opportunistic infections and Kaposi's sarcoma among a few Haitian refugees a national medical issue.[1]

1. See particularly Centers for Disease Control 1982a, 1982b, 1982c, 1982d; West 1983; Vieira et al. 1983. Between January 1981 and July 1982, Jeffrey Vieira and his colleagues analyzed the clinical and immunologic features of ten Haitian

With innuendoes, racist overtones, and inaccuracies, the popular press has described Haitian immigrants in the United States as illiterate, disease-ridden Voodoo practitioners, and has debated whether Haitians are political or economic refugees. Although much of the reporting is inconsistent and contradictory, it has nevertheless helped to make Haitian migration to the United States and especially the plight of the refugees in detention camps a national political issue. There is now an urgent need to reveal the story behind the newspaper and television accounts.

Unlike most of the other immigrant groups that came to the United States in search of employment or to escape political persecution in their native lands, Haitians started to arrive in large numbers only in the early 1960s. Their exodus, like that of Cuban refugees, was a flight from a dictatorial regime. While the majority of Cubans were welcomed as refugees and received considerable financial aid from the State Department, however, very few Haitians were granted such aid.

The problems that the Haitian population in the United States is facing are numerous and complex. The most heavily burdened with problems are the undocumented migrants. The number of undocumented Haitian immigrants has risen over the years. They live in constant fear of being identified, believing that, if deported, they may spend the rest of their lives in Haitian jails. This fear leads to stress-related emotional disorders and at the same time frequently keeps the immigrants from using the facilities of public hospitals. Instead, they rely on folk medicine to cure their ordinary ailments or seek out private clinics with Haitian medical personnel.

This book presents, from an anthropological perspective, an assessment of the development and socioeconomic adaptation of the Haitian community in New York City. Preliminary research for this project was carried out in Haiti during the summers of 1975 and 1976 and was financed by the Inter-American Institute of Ag-

---

patients with AIDS and opportunistic infections who were under treatment at Kings County Hospital–Downstate Medical Center in Brooklyn, New York. On the basis of their research, they reported that "the wide range of duration of residence before the onset of disease (three months to eight years) indicates that AIDS is not limited to Haitians who have recently immigrated" (Vieira et al. 1983:128).

ricultural Sciences of the Organization of American States and by the Fonds International de Coopération Universitaire through a grant administered by the Centre de Recherches Caraïbes of the University of Montreal, Canada. The second phase of the project was conducted from July 1977 to August 1978 among the Haitian community in New York City. This portion of the project was commissioned by the Institute for Social Research at Fordham University and by the Institute for Urban and Minority Education at Teachers College, Columbia University, and carried out under the auspices of the Research Institute for the Study of Man. The rewriting of the manuscript and its preparation for publication were made possible by a Faculty Research Grant and a Career Development Grant awarded to me in 1980 by the Research Board of the University of California at Berkeley.

Several friends and colleagues helped me in the preparation of this study. I owe a special debt to Joseph Fitzpatrick, chairman of the Committee on Migration Research at Fordham University, who arranged for me to do fieldwork among Haitian immigrants in New York. His friendship, advice, and extensive experience with the New York Caribbean community made it possible for me to complete this project. I also feel deep gratitude to Charles Harrington and Lambros Comitas, who invited me to join the Institute for Urban and Minority Education at Teachers College, Columbia University, encouraged me throughout the project, and were ready to help me whenever I needed them. The final preparation of the manuscript for publication owes much to suggestions and comments made by Roger Sanjek.

I am especially grateful to all of my informants who discussed with me the problems they encountered in New York City and in the process provided me with much of the information I needed to write this book. I especially single out the following compatriots: Paul and Franck Laraque, Max Manigat, Antoine Adrien, William Smarth, Franck Henry, Louis Brun, and Father Guy Sansaricq. They were very helpful to me during my stay in New York. Conversations and discussions with them gave me the opportunity to hear alternative views on numerous issues.

Many of the issues raised in this book were discussed at length in the course of a seminar on West Indian communities in the United States which I taught during the winter of 1978 at Fordham University and during the spring of 1979 and 1980 at the University of California at Berkeley. I am indebted to the students who participated in these seminars for their perceptive comments. Their pertinent questions made it possible for me to revise and clarify some of my earlier statements.

I have read most of the chapters in this book at academic meetings, colloquia, and symposia: Chapter 2 at the symposium "Caribbeans and the Shape of Their Future," organized by Hunter College of the City University of New York in the fall of 1977, and at the Wingspread Conference "Haiti: Present State and Future Prospects," sponsored by the Creole Institute of Indiana University and The Johnson Foundation in September 1982; Chapter 3 in the winter of 1978 as part of the lecture series sponsored by the Institute for Urban and Minority Education at Teachers College, Columbia University; Chapter 4, in adapted form, in the fall of 1980 at a conference on intrahemispheric migration sponsored and financed by the Institute of Latin American Studies at Rutgers University; Chapter 6 in the winter of 1979 in the Medical Anthropology Lecture Series at the University of California at Berkeley; and Chapter 7 in the fall of 1979 at the annual meeting of the American Anthropological Association in Cincinnati. I appreciate the comments of all who participated in those meetings.

I am grateful to several colleagues who read chapters of the manuscript in draft form and provided me with their insightful comments. The following were, in a special way, very helpful to me: Karen Bianchini; Roy Bryce-Laporte; George Bond; Leith Mullings; Janet Dolgin; Serge François, M.D.; Pierre Paul Antoine, M.D.; Constant Pierre-Louis, M.D.; Vera Rubin; Lydio and Silvano Tomasi; Susan Gould, R.N.; Roger Jean Charles, M.D.; Benjamin Siegel, M.D.; Eugene Hammel; Loretta Saint-Louis; Alan Harwood; and George De Vos. Their suggestions greatly improved the overall shape of the book.

I also thank the librarians of the following institutions for their help in locating materials pertaining to the history of Haitian migration to the United States: Bibliothèque Saint-Louis de Gonzague, Port-au-Prince; Research Institute for the Study of Man, New York; Columbia University Library; The New York Public Library; The Schomburg Collection in Black Culture, New York;

The Center for Migration Studies, Staten Island, New York; and the University of California Library at Berkeley.

This book incorporates material in some of my essays that have appeared elsewhere: "The Haitian Niche in New York City," *Migration Today* 7 (1979):12–18; "Haitian-Americans," in *Ethnicity and Medical Care*, edited by Alan Harwood (Cambridge: Harvard University Press, 1981), pp. 172–210; "Haitian Immigrants in the United States: A Historical Overview," in *White Collar Migrants in the Americas and the Caribbean*, edited by Arnaud F. Marks and Hebe M. C. Vessuri (Leiden: Royal Institute of Linguistics and Anthropology, 1983), pp. 119–69. I am grateful to the publishers indicated for permission to draw on this material here. I also express my heartfelt thanks to Walter H. Lippincott, Jr., and Barbara H. Salazar, both of Cornell University Press.

Finally, my gratitude goes to my graduate research assistant, Diane Peterson, for her editorial assistance, and to my secretaries, Cynthia Sharp and Elmirie Robinson-Cephas, for their dedicated work in the final preparation of the manuscript.

American Odyssey analyzes the social organization of the Haitian-American community within the larger context of Caribbean ethnicity and dependency. I hope the information it provides will help policy makers to ease the adaptation of the immigrants and will help Haitian-Americans themselves to integrate their communities with the structure of mainstream American society.

MICHEL S. LAGUERRE

Berkeley, California

AMERICAN ODYSSEY

HAITIANS IN NEW YORK CITY

[1]

The Migrants

Most of the Haitian immigrant population in the United States came here during the administrations of François Duvalier (1957–71) and his son, Jean-Claude, who succeeded him in 1971. The factors behind the migration include blatant political repression and the island's shrinking economy. Some people came to the United States directly, others after an interim stay in a third country.

The majority of the early immigrants were members of the upper and middle class in Haiti. They started to establish themselves here in the turbulent 1960s, when the United States was involved abroad in the Vietnam War and was troubled at home by the swelling protests of civil rights and black power activists against inequality in American society. The immigrants not only had fresh memories of the barbaric treatment they had been exposed to in Haiti, but also were fearful of being drafted to fight in Vietnam. Several young Haitian immigrants were indeed drafted and some were killed in action. It was in those circumstances that Haitian immigrants began to establish their ethnic community in New York City.

The wave of Haitian boat people entering the United States began only in 1972, one year after Jean-Claude Duvalier succeeded his father as president for life. These latest immigrants, who have arrived directly either from Haiti or from the Bahamas, tend to settle in the Miami metropolitan area.[1] A few of them, however,

1. For an overview of the problems that Haitian boat people face in Miami, see Walsh 1979.

have joined members of their families in New York and other American cities.

Over the past twenty years enclaves of Haitians have appeared in several American cities. Although the immigrants have come from various strata of Haitian society, they share many of the same cultural standards, the same languages (Creole and French), and the same mix of religions (French-influenced Catholicism, American-influenced evangelical Protestantism, and voodoo).

At present, Haitian immigrants can be found in almost every state. In such major cities as New York, Miami, Boston, Chicago, and Washington, D.C., Haitian communities form separate ecological niches.[2] Most have their own community churches, stores, restaurants, social and literary clubs, newspapers, physicians, and folk healers, all of which help the immigrants to maintain their cultural traditions. These communities are not isolated from one another. Through individual members, often relatives or in-laws, they maintain complex networks of communication, and internal migration for marriage or employment is sufficiently common to ensure that links between communities are maintained. By and large, the Haitian population in the United States is extremely diversified in terms of income structure, educational attainment, and skin color; class stratification within each community persists.

Although Haitian neighborhoods share various characteristics with other West Indian communities, they display their own cultural uniqueness, and the population brings its specific cultural contribution to New York's social life. Despite this contribution, very little is known about this recent immigrant community. Haitian immigrants have settled here quietly and have tried to maintain a low profile, not only because of the illegal status of some of them, but also as a result of the traumatic experiences they suffered in Haiti before they left the island.

New York was chosen as the site for this research for several reasons. It has a larger concentration of Haitian and other West Indian immigrants than any other American locality.[3] I agree with

2. A few theses and doctoral dissertations have been written on Haitian immigrants in New York City and Evanston, Illinois. See, for example, Glick 1975, Buchanan 1980, Woldemikael 1980, Poux 1973, Clérismé 1974, and R. E. Marshall 1974.

3. The terms "West Indian" and "Caribbean" are used interchangeably in this book to refer to immigrants from the Caribbean islands. In some contexts Haitian

Roy Bryce-Laporte (1979:215) that "even conceding the unique geographical and transportational functions of Miami relative to the Caribbean regions, New York remains the leading target and *entrepôt* [port of entry] for Caribbean peoples to the United States." It is at the community level that the interactions between immigrants and their environment can best be observed and analyzed (see Holmes 1978:18, Rex 1973).

The Haitian population of New York covers a wide range of immigrant status. Some are naturalized American citizens; others have a legal immigrant or nonimmigrant status; some are undocumented aliens and refugees; and still others are children born in this country of Haitian parents. Among the legal nonimmigrants are students, temporary workers, tourists, Haitian government personnel, and employees of international organizations. Among the undocumented aliens are people who overstayed the length of time their visas allowed them and others who came here without U.S. visas. There is also a category of individuals with transitional status: people who have requested political asylum and whose cases are still pending, and those who are in the process of legalizing their immigrant status through marriage with American citizens or through other channels.

Migration Then and Now

Although Haitians migrated sporadically to the United States in the nineteenth century, no significant immigration occurred during that period, largely because of the institutionalized racial discrimination that prevailed in the United States (Souffrant 1974: 133–45). The first significant group of Haitian migrants, about 500 upper-class urban families, came to the United States in the 1920s. Fleeing the atrocities that accompanied the American occupation of Haiti from 1915 to 1934,[4] these families settled among

immigrants identify themselves as either West Indians or Caribbeans, in others as Haitians.

4. During the American occupation of Haiti peasants were forced to work without pay building public roads (Castor 1971). Several nationalist leaders, among them Charlemagne Péralte, as well as some of their supporters and followers were killed by U.S. marines. These leaders organized various *kako* (guerrilla) groups throughout the island in an effort to liberate the republic from the American occupation.

black Americans in Harlem and have since been assimilated into the mainstream of American society (Reid 1939:97).

The Haitian population that will occupy our attention here has come to the United States since 1957, when François Duvalier was elected president of Haiti.[5] In that year defeated presidential candidates and their close collaborators fled the country and developed a political base in New York City with the intention of organizing guerrilla troops to invade the island. They did in fact launch several invasions, but none of them succeeded in overthrowing Papa Doc's regime. By 1964, when François Duvalier was elected president for life, most expatriate politicians realized that their chances of returning to Haiti were at best slim and began to send for their relatives. Many of these people, however, have continued their efforts to organize revolutionary opposition to the Duvalier regime.

Since Papa Doc's death in 1971, economic deprivation and political repression have been the major factors behind the emigration of both urbanites and peasants. Groups of these migrants, unable to gather the funds necessary to secure Haitian passports and United States visas, have been coming to this country covertly in small boats. Risking their lives on long journeys on the high seas, some have died during the passage, and others have been jailed upon arrival in the United States for illegal entry (U.S. Congress, House, 1976).

The Demographic Picture

The Haitian population of the United States in the early 1980s is estimated to number about 800,000, including the American-born children of immigrants.[6] Because of the sizable undocumented

5. During this same period, many Haitians emigrated to Canada (Déjean 1978, Jadotte 1977), Cuba (Diaz 1973), France (Bastide et al. 1974), the Dominican Republic (Bajeux 1973), Zaire (Dorsinville 1973), and the Bahamas (D. I. Marshall 1979). Some of them later emigrated to the United States.

6. The estimate of 800,000 immigrants of Haitian descent in the United States was arrived at through a series of encounters with knowledgeable Haitian community leaders and my interpretation of official data in the annual reports issued by the Immigration and Naturalization Service. The estimated Haitian emigration of 0.4 percent per year issued by the World Bank (1979) was also taken into consideration. No reliable national or local census data are available on the undocumented Haitian immigrant population.

population, however, there is no way of knowing the exact population figures. Estimates provide the following breakdown: approximately 150,000 are either American citizens or permanent residents; about 200,000 are children of both legal and undocumented immigrants who were born in the United States and are therefore American citizens; approximately 50,000 hold student or other visas that allow them to remain legally in the United States; and roughly 400,000 are undocumented entrants. Among this last group, 75,000 persons are estimated to be in the process of becoming permanent residents either by marrying American residents or citizens or by other means.

The annual reports issued by the INS, which deal exclusively with the legal population, permit some observations about the demography of this sector of Haitian-Americans. From 1962 to 1975, 63,642 Haitians were admitted to the United States as legal immigrants. Although they have settled in almost every state of the Union, the vast majority (72 percent of all legal immigrants in 1975) are concentrated in New York State, primarily in New York City.[7] Minor concentrations occur in Illinois, Florida, Massachusetts, and New Jersey.

In comparison with the total United States population, the age distribution of legally admitted Haitian immigrants is disproportionately weighted in the age range of 10 to 19 years. (Annually between 1970 and 1975, 19 to 36 percent of legal immigrants were teenagers.) Female immigrants slightly outnumber males (53 and 47 percent, respectively). Extensive observations of the Haitian population in New York have led me to the conclusion that the sex ratio of the legal population is representative of the undocumented population as well. This situation can be explained in part by the fact that the U.S. Consulate in Haiti has been more lenient in providing tourist visas to Haitian women than to Haitian men. For, unlike Mexican migrants, a large proportion of Haitians who are here illegally came as tourists with American visas and stayed on.

Migrants have come from nearly every city, village, hamlet, and rural district in Haiti. Nevertheless, Port-au-Prince has been the

7. Most Caribbean immigrants settle in New York. Ransford Palmer (1976:45) has found that "seventy-three percent of all Caribbean immigrants in the United States in 1970 lived in the New York City Metropolitan area and comprised the second largest group in that area."

main provider of émigrés, not only because massive migration started with Port-au-Prince residents but also because every person who wishes to emigrate legally is likely to have spent some time in Port-au-Prince while securing a Haitian passport and U.S. visa. Thus almost all Haitian migrants (except the boat people who have settled in Miami) acquired some experience of city life before they emigrated.

The problems that the Haitian immigrant population faces in developing an ethnic enclave and subculture, maintaining its cultural traditions, strengthening its links with the motherland, and interacting with the wider society are similar to those commonly experienced by other immigrant groups. Yet the structure of racial discrimination that permeates every aspect of American life and the cultural traditions of the immigrants have a tremendous bearing on the process of their integration in American society.

Haitian-Americans as an Ethnic Group

The notion of ethnicity, with all of its social, economic, and political implications, is central to an analysis of the structural position and internal social organization of the Haitian community in New York City. As a conceptual tool, ethnicity is multivocal; for that reason it can be used on the one hand to decode a wide range of cultural symbols and on the other hand to unveil the structural position of an immigrant and ethnic community.

Some studies of ethnic groups have emphasized their internal structuring and the external forces that define their boundaries (Barth 1969:14). Such an approach defines ethnicity in the context of conflict theory. Ethnic groups are seen as "interest groups" (Glazer and Moynihan 1970; Glazer and Moynihan, eds., 1975). They are said to provide a cultural context and base that enable their members to struggle and compete for material resources and power (Furnivall 1948; M. G. Smith 1965; Despres 1967; Despres, ed., 1975). From an internal colonial perspective, they are also seen as victims of discriminatory policies of national governments geared toward ethnocide (Whitten 1975, Yette 1971). In its less politicized form the emphasis on the group aspect of ethnicity has also led some scholars to focus on the assimilation process of ethnic groups in the host society and on the new identities they are about to develop (Gordon 1964, Fitzpatrick 1971).

The group aspect of ethnicity is sometimes minimized in order to emphasize the individual aspect. In the words of Stanford Lyman and William Douglass (1973:349), "from the ethnic actor's perspective, ethnicity is both a mental state and a potential ploy in any encounter, but it will be neither if it cannot be invoked or activated." At the individual level, ethnicity is seen as a game people play to display their ethnic membership and to take advantage of particular personal situations. The emphasis on the "cognitive dimension of ethnicity" is to draw attention to alternatives that exist "in the situational selection of ethnic identity" (Handelman 1977:188). Members of ethnic groups tend to manipulate their ethnicity "to advance their personal interests and maximize their power" (A. Cohen, ed., 1974:xiii).

The group and individual aspects of ethnicity are not contradictory, but rather complementary. Ethnicity can no longer be understood as an abstraction; it has a situational context, as Joan Vincent indicates when she writes (1974:376) that "a complete definition of ethnicity is first structural . . . and second, situational—the content of ethnic interaction being related to the specific situation."

Ethnicity must be defined in terms of its internal structuring and the external forces that impinge upon it. To understand it properly, one must take into consideration the structural elements that are quintessential to the makeup of an ethnic community: the three membership categories of the people who form the group. Membership in an ethnic group can be ascribed, self-ascribed, or pro-ascribed. Membership is *ascribed* when one belongs to the group through birth. In such a situation, individuals are socialized within the group and learn to identify with it. They develop a sense of belonging to the group (De Vos and Romanucci-Ross, eds., 1975). Self-ascribed membership may occur either through affinal and fictive kinship ties with ascribed members of the group or through personal choice. A wife who belongs to an ethnic group other than her husband's may find it advantageous to identify herself with her husband's group. A sizable number of people occupy the self-ascribed category. Some Dominican immigrants in New York, for example, prefer to identify themselves as Puerto Ricans and thus avoid the harassment of immigration agents. As Lyman and Douglass (1973:358) put it, "identity switching is a common tactic when the particular identity of the actor becomes distinctly disadvantageous and another seems to promise better pay-offs in the encounter." Finally, membership in an ethnic group can be pro-ascribed or assigned by others. Government reports, for example, usually count Haitians, Jamaicans, and Trinidadians as black Americans, pro-ascribing West Indian immigrants to membership in Afro-American communities. Similarly, when a crime is committed by a Spanish-speaking person in New York, it is often automatically assumed that the perpetrator is Puerto Rican.

Ethnicity is often used as an adaptive strategy by which individuals and groups define themselves and are defined by others in situational relationships within the context of a structure of dependence and inequality (Laguerre 1979d). It is also used as a ploy to define status differences and enhance class interests. Symbolic and cultural aspects of ethnicity, through which one glorifies and maintains one's cultural tradition, are secondary to its most important characteristic—class consciousness leading to the contextual use of ethnicity for purposes of social and economic mobility. I suggest that class consciousness defines the content and sets the boundaries within which variability in the manifestation and manipulation of ethnicity can be achieved.

Haitian ethnicity in New York is expressed not in a vacuum but within the realm of the social class to which one belongs. The demarcation of social classes in the community often reflects the experience of the immigrants in their homeland. The immigrants' generation or migration experience, however, is also an important factor.

Haitian-Americans as the Media See Them

Little reporting in the press about Haitian-Americans fails to make sensationalist statements about their voodoo practices. Voodoo has been evoked for its mysterious rituals, its exotic beliefs, its lascivious dances, and its criminal practices. Edward Tivnan (1979:15) has pointed out that "Voodoo has always suffered from a bad press: reports of grave robbers arrested with skulls headed for 'Voodoo rites,' 'Voodoo ladies' blessing the guns and drugs of heroin dealers; chicken carcasses in Riverside Park; bloody bits of goat by a Central Park transverse road; a decapitated rooster in Prospect Park; a ram's head drifting in the Harlem Meer." Such innuendoes about voodoo-related crimes have never been proved to have any empirical basis. In fact, the community affairs officer of the 77th Precinct in Brooklyn, located in the midst of a very densely populated Haitian-American neighborhood, is reported to have said in 1979: "In my 26 years here, I have never come across any crime actually linked to Voodoo. Narcotics is still our biggest problem in this area" (*New York Times Magazine*, December 2, 1979).

Voodoo is basically a religion and healing system developed by slaves during the colonial period. It is the result of a syncretism between African ethnotheologies and Christian and Amerindian religions within the context of the plantation system (Laguerre 1980b). It is a religion with its theological doctrines, moral principles, hierarchical clergy, devout congregation, and liturgical rituals, one not so different from similar syncretistic religions found among other New Yorkers, especially the Cubans, Puerto Ricans, and various immigrant groups from elsewhere in Latin America.

I have observed voodoo rituals in homes in New York and Miami. According to a report in the *New York Times Magazine* of December 2, 1979, "no one can say for sure how many New Yorkers are members of Voodoo or santería sects, but 'thousands' is a common estimate of those in or familiar with the religions." In my judgment, there is no way one can know at present the exact numbers of voodoo priests, priestesses, healers, and practitioners because many of the participants are undocumented aliens and are wary of revealing their identity.

Press reports on the Haitians' language have been very confusing. Since French is the official language of Haiti, it is sometimes reported that the Haitian immigrants are a French-speaking people. This is a myth widely shared among New Yorkers and in some agencies and public facilities that deal with Haitian immigrants. The fact is that only the educated elite in Haiti speak French, and they are fluent in Creole as well. The great majority of Haitians speak only Creole. Creole is not bastard French; it is a distinct language with its own grammar, morphology, and syntax, which originated during the colonial period through the acculturation of

African slaves with each other and with European planters. "Haitian Creole is already the second most common foreign language (next to Spanish) in the New York City public school system" (USAID 1980:3).

The Haitian population of New York City is not only geographically dispersed but also socioeconomically heterogeneous (Glick 1975). New York Haitians generally regard Manhattan as the borough where middle-class Haitian families live, Brooklyn as lower class, and Queens as upper middle class. My own observations do not support these perceptions; people of the various strata are found in all three boroughs. Migrants from particular Haitian villages and cities do tend to cluster in the same boroughs, however; Queens, for example, has a concentration of light-skinned migrants from Jérémie, a city in the south of Haiti, and many natives of Lascahobas, a village on the central plateau of Haiti, live in Brooklyn. This pattern of settlement by area of origin helps immigrants to adapt to the city's demands and ensures that someone nearby can be called upon in time of illness or other crisis.

It is nevertheless important to note that people who live in any one of these enclaves maintain ongoing relationships with friends and relatives in other enclaves and in other boroughs. Medical problems of Brooklyn Haitians, for example, are sometimes treated by medical practitioners in Manhattan or Queens. Indeed, the extent and intensity of ties among people residing in different enclaves make the Haitian population in New York City a single dispersed community. When a family member falls ill, friends and relatives from other boroughs show up to help diagnose and cure the patient or recommend a physician or folk healer.

The Haitian population is not at all homogeneous in its medical beliefs and practices. The medical traditions of migrants from rural districts of Haiti or from such outlying islands as Ile de la Tortue, Ile à Vache, and Ile de la Gonâve, who were accustomed to seek the aid of folk healers rather than physicians, differ from those of Port-au-Prince intellectuals, who may have been educated in France and had little contact with folk medicine. In any case, city people in general are more receptive to and knowledgeable about scientific medicine than rural people. Thus one's social class, education, residential background, and skin color help to predict one's health practices.

Researching the Haitian Community in New York

The boroughs of Brooklyn, Manhattan, and Queens were selected for this study because of the large numbers of Haitian immigrants who live there. New York City has the largest concentration of individuals of Haitian extraction in the United States, roughly 450,000.[8] The fiercest opponents of the Duvalier administration are here, and in fact almost every Haitian living in the United States has a relative or close friend in New York.[9] In New York more than in any other American city, Haitians display their cultural distinctiveness through a network of churches, private businesses, and voluntary associations. It is not surprising to hear individuals speaking Creole in the subway between Manhattan and Brooklyn; to find migrants congregating in a voodoo priest's home to perform voodoo ceremonies on Saturday evenings; to hear Haitian music and news during "Haitian hours" on four radio stations based in New York; and to learn every week in the Haitian-American-owned newspapers that a Haitian political meeting or cultural event is being held somewhere in the city. These are some of the factors that make New York City the appropriate place in which to conduct this kind of study.

When I arrived in New York City in July 1977, I visited friends and relatives, explaining to them the kind of research I wanted to carry out in the Haitian community there. They provided me with much offhand information and advice about people with whom I should speak, and made arrangements for me to see friends of theirs who they believed were knowledgeable about the conditions of Haitians in the city. Through this friendship base, I developed a network of informants from various strata of the New York Haitian community in a relatively short time. While I was pooling

8. To put this figure in perspective, in 1975 the total population of Haiti was estimated at 5,399,373 inhabitants, 2,699,860 males and 2,699,513 females (Institut Haïtien de Statistique 1976:48). A World Bank report estimates the Port-au-Prince population at 653,000 and the total urban population at 1,079,000 in the same year. A 1981 report of USAID estimated the total population at 6 million, with an annual population growth rate of 1.8 percent. According to this report, 24 percent of the population live in urban areas and 76 percent in rural areas (USAID 1981).

9. Teklemarian Woldemikael (1980:136) has made a similar observation in reference to Haitian immigrants in Evanston: "They also have relatives and friends all over the United States, particularly in New York."

all kinds of information to gain a sense of the community needs, I also read all the relevant literature I could find in the city's public and university libraries.

Between August 1977 and June 1978, I interviewed informants from the various social classes both intensively and informally. Through these interviews, I was able to gather substantive data on family organization, employment patterns, political participation, and health practices. Group interviews were also conducted. The group setting had the advantage of allowing contradictory views on the same subject to be voiced and discussed. All of the interviews were conducted in Haitian Creole. I usually started by explaining the nature of the questions and topics in which I was interested and then let the informants talk freely. When they felt they had exhausted the subject, I posed specific questions and asked for clarification and additional commentary.

Extended interviews were also conducted with health professionals, some in private practice and others on the staffs of various public, private, and proprietary hospitals. These interviews focused on the particular kinds of medical ailments that these health-care providers treat among Haitians in New York. Hospital staff members who act as interpreters for Haitian patients of non-Creole-speaking physicians were also helpful in this regard. Additional interviews with former patients acquainted me with the types of illnesses they incurred and the extent to which they continued to use folk medicine.

My data on health practices were derived mainly from lower-class respondents and from observations of the health behavior of mainly lower-income patients by Haitian physicians and other middle-class Haitian-Americans. Although educated Haitians and the mulatto elite were quite ready to express their ideas about the health-care behavior of impoverished or uneducated Haitians, they were less ready to talk about their own behavior, which they (like most elites) consider to be no one's business but their own.

[2]

The Ecological Context of Haitian Emigration

The socioeconomic adaptation of the Haitian community in New York City cannot be understood in all of its ramifications without a proper comprehension of the ecological context of Haitian emigration. By means of chain migration and various group-centered strategies, New York immigrants manage to pay the passage of kin who might otherwise find it difficult, because of Haiti's present political and economic situation, to emigrate to the United States.[1] The emigration of Haitians is a long process structured within the total ecology of the home island. The notion of total ecology here includes infrastructural as well as superstructural forces that determine migration patterns. It takes into consideration relationships of individuals to the physical environment in terms of available resources, the social atmosphere of the locale as shaped by social interactions, and the dependency ideology from which arises the migration ideology so characteristic of Haitians. Using a symbolic interactionist approach within the context of a transactional analysis, I analyze in this chapter the role of migrants as players in a risky game that they do not fully understand, but which they expect to win.[2]

1. For an in-depth discussion of this issue, see MacDonald and MacDonald 1964 and Laguerre 1978a.

2. For further elaboration on the symbolic interactionist approach in the sociological literature, see Bales 1950; Blumer 1969; Goffman 1967, 1972.

Migration Ideology

Haitians would not seek to migrate to New York City if they did not have some idea that their project could be realized. Migration ideology is the thought process by which an individual perceives the possibility of moving from one place to another in order to achieve stated personal goals.[3] People often see the world as divided into centers and peripheries. In this perspective, internal/external migration is nothing less than an attempt to move from a position on the periphery to a place at the center, where one can basically enjoy a better social environment, employment, and sometimes political security.

From the perspective of dependency theory, Haitian migrants differ little from other migrants. The Haitian case is unique, however, in the configuration of variables that make it possible for migrants to develop an ideology consistent with the geographical position and the dependent status of the island and to develop productive adaptive strategies that enable them to reach their goals. Because Haitian emigration to New York City was very light until 1957, when François Duvalier was elected president of Haiti, this analysis will focus mainly on migration trends from the early 1960s up to the present.

In addition to the acute and seemingly permanent political and economic crisis in Haiti, several secondary factors contribute to the choice of New York as the particularly cherished destination. Here I shall concentrate not on the structural push and pull factors that are at play in any mass migration, but rather on reactions of individuals to these phenomena, especially their internalization of a migration ideology. The idea of migrating to New York may come when one has a relative or a friend who already lives there. When immigrants send money and pictures of their apartments and their families to their relatives and friends back home, those people come to realize that New York provides great economic opportunities. This feedback and communication may serve as a stimulus for emigration. And, when a migrant returns home for a visit, relatives and friends become aware that the New York visitor

3. A clarification of the notion of migration ideology is provided in Philpott 1973.

is doing well, in fact is better off economically than they are. If the visitor tells about difficult living conditions, hard work in a factory, and violence in the New York subways, they may prefer to ignore such stories if they are convinced that life is better in New York than in Haiti. Similar observations have also been made in the case of Dominican migrants (Hendricks 1974).

The idea of emigrating to New York may also arise during a rural person's first visit to Port-au-Prince. The Port-au-Prince environment is crucial to this process. New York is a very popular topic of conversation among its residents, and, from time to time immigrants visit their former neighbors, relate their experiences, and offer advice on arrangements for leaving the country. In Port-au-Prince one may establish contacts with people who are important to the success of this endeavor—travel agents and immigration officials.

Individuals may embrace a migration ideology through their own quest for a better life. Often, though, the family or a relative in New York decides that it would be good for one of them to leave the island. In any case, one must internalize the ideology, making it one's own, in order to decide to migrate and to take the necessary steps to achieve that goal.

Internalizing a migration ideology, however, is not enough; one must be able to secure the necessary funds to make the trip a reality. To do so, the extended family—sometimes both in Haiti and in the United States—must become involved financially or otherwise. Decisions as to who will attempt to migrate are made primarily within the extended family.

Migration Selectivity

Some steps that follow underlying grammatical rules must be taken to ensure the success of the migration project. Certain strategies must be developed to guarantee the highest probability of success in order to avoid frustration, economic loss, and failure. Migration selectivity is the first step in that process.[4]

4. For an alternative view on migration selectivity, see Jackson, ed., 1969.

A decision to migrate must receive the approval of other members of the extended family. Often a family member will not attempt to migrate if another member appears to have a better chance of success. By and large, lower-class Haitians believe that the people who are most likely to migrate successfully and therefore present the least risk are educated men (unmarried or married), young people (capable of securing student visas), and unmarried women. The person most likely to be approved by the entire family is the one considered eventually to be able to pay for the passage of other kin to New York. During the administration of Papa Doc, the family was not interested in investing much money in former members of the military and the police corps because the government, afraid that such men might be recruited by political groups in New York to launch an invasion of the island, refused them exit visas.

The selection of a person to migrate may also be made by a relative in New York. A New York Haitian who has dependent relatives in Haiti may persuade and help them to come to New York in the hope of escaping the burden of supporting a nuclear-family unit in Haiti. If dependent relatives can be brought to New York, they can be expected to take care of themselves.

Family members in Haiti sometimes arrange marriages for relatives abroad. A man in New York who despairs of finding a virgin to marry, or who finds Haitian women in the United States too liberated for his taste, may ask his kin in Haiti to find him a wife of good family and morals there. The marriage can be arranged before the two persons even meet. The man then goes back to the island for the wedding. Later the wife applies to the U.S. Consulate for immigrant status in order to join her husband in New York. This kind of marital arrangement is referred to as *mariag bay bous* or *mariag djet*, that is, a marriage that makes a prospective applicant eligible for permanent resident status in the United States.

What is clear in the selection process is the interaction of three points in a triangle: the individual migrant-to-be, members of the extended family in Haiti, and a friend or relative abroad. To ensure the success of the project, each person involved in this network provides the individual with much advice and financial aid. At this stage, the individual is likely to realize that he or she is not alone in this enterprise and can rely on family members and friends for help. Family support is central to the success of such a project.

Family Cooperation

Haitian migration has its own grammar, morphology, and syntax that underlie the various steps of the migration ritual. Before migrating to New York, an individual must participate in an informal family meeting to map out strategies. At this informal gathering the would-be migrant discusses the resources available for the project. The family members may decide to pool their money for the project unless a relative in New York agrees to pay the expenses. To meet the challenge, the family members may have to sell some of their property—a horse, some other animals, a few acres of land—or they may borrow from a friend abroad. If the enterprise fails, the money may be lost forever.

Older folk are consulted about the best ways to sell property and about what to sell first. The most resourceful person will accompany the migrant to a travel agency. A knowledgeable friend may act as intermediary or oversee the process to prevent the travel agent from exploiting the migrant.

The family offers emotional support. The would-be migrant who does not live in Port-au-Prince must make frequent visits to the city, and the family members ask from time to time if any progress is being made and offer their encouragement and their prayers. The family may start a novena to ensure the success of the project or make a promise to a Catholic saint or a voodoo spirit. The migrant may be asked to make a pilgrimage to a shrine on the island, to start going to mass on Sundays, or to see a voodoo priest for a *bain chance*, a voodoo bath for luck. In some cases, a voodoo priest may tell the supplicant that no payment is expected unless the project is successful. The supplicant usually understands that he or she eventually will be expected to pay the voodoo priest's passage to New York.

It is also the duty of family members to ask their friends in government service to help in any way they can to secure a passport and perhaps a U.S. visa. The family makes sure that nothing is left to chance. From the time of the inception of the project until the person leaves the island, the entire family experiences great stress. Their money is being used, and they have no guarantee that the journey will be made. If it is not, the project may be a total economic loss for the entire family.[5]

The Role of Port-au-Prince

To migrate legally from Haiti to New York, one must generally pass through Port-au-Prince. But there are many other reasons for going to Port-au-Prince, and they can lead indirectly to a person's decision to emigrate. As there are relatively few high schools in the countryside, an elementary school graduate is likely to go to Port-au-Prince to attend high school and perhaps the State University of Haiti.[6] A high school student in Port-au-Prince is likely to develop a network of friends who can be helpful, and is in a position to acquire a proper understanding of migration channels and to make a realistic appraisal of the entire process.

Some eventual migrants go to the city in search of work—unemployment in the countryside is very high—and end up enlarging the urban population.[7] Still others go to get proper vocational training in order to have a diploma to show at the U.S. Consulate when they apply for a visa. Some domestics, previously recruited to work for Port-au-Prince families who then migrated to New York, have their plane tickets paid for by their former employers. Domestics usually develop close personal relationships with the children in the families they serve, and after the children arrive in New York they may beg their parents to send for the domestics. Some children send their own money to such domestics to pay for their passage in installments.

A good number of people in Haiti dream of the day when they can migrate to New York. Port-au-Prince has become a transit place for most of them in a kind of stage migration (Mangin 1967:79). A peasant who decides to migrate to New York will go

5. The role of the extended family in Haitian migration is discussed in Laguerre 1978b and 1978c.

6. See Laguerre 1979c for an ethnography of schooling in Haiti.

7. Two studies (Fass 1978, Laguerre 1982a) have discussed at length the ecology of urban poverty in Haiti.

first to Port-au-Prince to become accustomed to city ways, to learn some English, to start transactions with a travel agent, to develop a network of contacts, and finally to apply for an exit visa from the Haitian government and an American visa from the U.S. Consulate.

Not all migrants from the countryside take up temporary residence in Port-au-Prince while preparing their immigration papers. Some prefer not to let their neighbors know about their migration plans, so they travel back and forth to the city to arrange for their papers. An individual who wants to avoid unwelcome questions, is unable to pay a debt before leaving the island, or fears interference in the project will follow such a policy.

The stay in Port-au-Prince was crucial in the 1960s, when it was a question of *non monté, non dėsand*: each application for an exit visa is judged according to its own merit. Names of migrants were sent to the National Palace to be checked by François Duvalier's advisers, and migrants had to appear every day at the Haitian Immigration Office to find out if the president had approved their departure. Under Jean-Claude Duvalier, names are no longer closely screened, and the process of getting an exit visa is a bit simpler. One still has to wait a long time, however, and make multiple visits to a travel agency before one can obtain a passport.

The Travel Agent as Middleman

With the advent of the Duvalier family to the Presidential Palace, travel agencies have become some of the most popular establishments in Port-au-Prince. For the vast majority of illiterate people who wish to leave the country, the travel agent has become a crucial figure. He is a broker and a middleman in the multifaceted process of obtaining a passport, an exit visa, and one of the three types of U.S. visa (tourist, permanent resident, student).

The travel agent's role is most crucial in helping clients build a strategy for visa eligibility. The tangle of U.S. immigration laws and visa requirements makes the process quite difficult (see Glick 1975:59–63).[8] To obtain a permanent resident visa one generally

8. See Gonzalez 1971 on the Dominican Republic.

needs an offer of a job from an American employer. The low-paying jobs that an immigrant is most likely to find, however, are not officially eligible; thus this type of visa is rarely obtained by anyone other than the highly skilled professional. To obtain a tourist visa one must show proof of ability to support oneself during one's stay and a round-trip ticket as evidence of one's intention to return. These rules may require the would-be migrant to raise $1,500 or more. A student with a letter of acceptance from an American school must likewise show proof of support. Thus for the great majority of Haitians, the process of migrating to the United States is a formidable challenge that requires the operation of a complex sociopolitical mechanism. And the hand that operates the controls of the mechanism is, for the most part, that of the travel agent.

For the illiterate as well as for others, the travel agent fills out forms, develops the necessary strategies for visa eligibility, helps translate documents, and secures passports and exit visas. He inspects birth certificates to make sure that he does not enter a nonregistered name on the forms. He establishes personal contacts with employees of the consulate and the immigration office. He must have contacts in the Internal Revenue Service, in the national archives, and at police headquarters as well. He has assistants whom he introduces to these contacts, and the assistants do the real work of visiting the various offices to pick up passports and other papers. The travel agent's network of contacts allows him to accomplish these tasks with some degree of efficiency.

The agent also collects the various documents needed by the applicant. Depending on the type of strategy he is using, he may request papers proving ownership of land or a shop, a house certificate, a diploma (high school or vocational), checks or bank records, a letter of invitation from a relative abroad, a letter of guarantee of return from an official if the person is a government employee, and so on.

Having obtained the necessary documents, the travel agent must also do what is called *fè bouch moun yo*, that is, teach the individual what to say to the consul. He may go over a series of routine questions and provide sample answers for each. The individual must be able to satisfy the consul that he or she is entitled to a visa. With his past experience in the business, the travel agent is in a good position to determine the best strategies and to obtain the guarantees that the consul may request.

Three types of travel agent operate in Port-au-Prince: *bon ajan*, a licensed agent who has an office where he can be consulted; *ajan nan la ri*, an agent who has no office and no license, but operates with the help of a government official; *ajan met dam* or *ajan souflantiou*, an unlicensed agent who is an extension of a licensed agent. The *souflantiou* may get a few clients and channel them to the *bon ajan*. The latter will take no responsibility for the client, but will do the proper work and receive some money from his *souflantiou* associates. Among the *ajan nan la ri* are a few students from the lycées of Port-au-Prince who have friends among government employees. They pay no taxes, for they are not registered as travel agents.

Travel agents acquire their clientele through their own strategies and through recommendations from people in Haiti or abroad. To stay in the business, an agent must have runners who find prospective clients through friends and by checking gossip leads. A runner receives a commission for each client he brings to the agency, part of the lump sum the client has to pay for a passport.

The success of a travel agent depends greatly on his past performance, the length of time he has been in the business, his reliability, the kinds of contacts he has been able to maintain with government officials and the U.S. Consulate and *pratik* (clientele) ties he has been able to establish with families in Port-au-Prince. He must make himself known in the city and in the countryside. To this end, he may make a special effort to obtain visas for a few people in outlying districts. An agent who obtains a visa for someone in an outlying area becomes popular there. He may show up in the consulate and say hello to an official so that the people present can see that he has contacts there. He may ask a local radio station to announce his upcoming trip to New York to visit relatives, and the local newspapers to write something about his return and the length of time he spent abroad, as tactics to attract business.

The travel agent's role is enhanced by the nature of Haitian society and the complexity of its bureaucracy. As soon as an individual becomes an officeholder in the Port-au-Prince government, he places a wall between himself and the common people. The only way they can interact with him is through a broker. The agent is not easily accessible, either; one may need another broker to see him. The country is run from top to bottom on the principle not of the common good but of *moun pa*, nepotism; one must resort to *maniget*, the use of contacts, to get something done.

The Migrant in the Liminal Period

Emotional and Psychological Stress

From the inception of the migration project, the migrant experiences the emotional and psychological stress of a threefold pressure. First, a large amount of money, perhaps the economic base of the extended family, is being put at risk. Any bad luck may mean the family's economic ruin. Second, the procedures necessary to secure a passport and a visa are stressful. The migrant must pay many visits to the travel agency, where, almost without exception, the agent and his staff will not tell the entire truth. One must wait seemingly endlessly to learn the result of a process one does not fully understand. Third, no matter how ardently migration is sought, it promises to separate the migrant from family, friends, and country. It also entails responsibilities. If the enterprise should succeed, how is the migrant to reimburse the family members who remain at home? If promises have been made, can the migrant realistically expect to be able to keep them?

The migrant becomes the center of family attention, perhaps for the first time. This situation may be somewhat embarrassing. For the first time, one may be made aware of the general problems of the family. For the first time, one may receive weekly briefings about the family situation and may develop new dyadic relationships with kin. People behave as though one were about to disappear forever.

The migrant worries about life in New York. Everyone has heard contradictory statements about it from visitors. One can be sure, however, about the kinds of problem that will be forever left behind: political insecurity and poverty. From observing the behavior of visitors from New York, the migrant has come to realize that there are great possibilities for economic improvement there. The idea of owning a car, a television set, and a home is appealing to one who can never expect to have those things in Haiti.

Encounter Interactions

Most lower-class Haitians have a certain image of the travel agent and the U.S. consul before interacting with them. The image develops from rumors and gossip and much folklore, and it is a negative one. The travel agent is seen as a crook whose business is to get as much money as he can from a migrant. He is seen as a liar, an exploiter, someone on whom one cannot rely. The American consul is perceived as a person who cannot be trusted, one who has been put in the consulate for the sole purpose of saying no to Haitians. This negative image does not help one to play the role one is expected to play before both individuals: that of being secure and confident enough to convince both that one is entitled to migrate because of one's knowledge of U.S. requirements and one's ability to meet them.

The migrant's idea of the travel agent typically develops through gossip. Everyone has heard about someone whose money and time were wasted on a travel agent who failed to deliver a visa. One fears the same fate when one is asked to return again and again to the agency. This is a major problem in agent-client interactions. The client does not realize how much time must be allowed to obtain a passport. Because of the torpor of the Port-au-Prince bureaucracy, the agent needs at least two weeks to get a passport; but in order not to lose his client, he may say he expects to have it in a day or two. Sometimes this is a good strategy. If the agent needs more documents, the person will be able to supply them. The migrant, however, will be asked to show up every other day for about a month. One usually will not be able to see the agent himself, only his assistants. Frustration starts at this early stage. The agent himself does not know how long the job will take, because he depends on his assistants, who in turn depend on government employees to process the papers. A successful agent will always have an encouraging word (*ajan-ki gin bon bouch*) for his client, counseling patience. But he will not explain the process, for fear the client may believe that he is not efficient and go to see another agent, who may untruthfully claim he can do the job in a week.

One basic problem in the social distance between the agent and the client is the client's typical unwillingness to speak openly. Most clients are loath to say that they have sufficient funds to pay for their passage for fear of inciting the agent's greed for more money. There is an atmosphere of *sous-entendu*, in which agent and client speak more in metaphor than in explicit language. They are supposed to understand each other; usually, in fact, they do not.

The migrant's nervousness before the agent and the consul do not improve matters. The client trusts neither of them, and a great deal of money is at stake. A Brooklyn informant said rightly that anyone who visits the consul is part of a three-unit social field—*échec devan-l, li nan mitan, réalité-a dè yèl*: one contemplates the failure of the project, leaves behind all social reality, and finds oneself in between.

Sometimes the consul tries to speak Creole in an effort to make himself understood, and the migrant may try to speak French for the same purpose. The resulting confusion leads to the refusal of many visas. The confrontation with the consul is a kind of game with two players, each trying to win through questioning, answering, and self-presentation. The time of year and the consul's experience with Haitian migrants are also factors that may either militate against or help the migrant to secure a visa. The interaction procedures between the consul and the migrant are partly shaped by Haitian culture, which encourages politeness, nonaggressiveness, respect for authority, and patience in the face of God's will. For the migrant, interaction is based not on a struggle for one's rights, but rather on the exercise of forbearance while waiting for a person in authority to decide one's fate.

The U.S. Consulate is the only place in Haiti where peasants and city people, rich and poor alike, continually share the same ecological space. In 1975 and 1976 I saw people start to form lines in front of the consulate at 4:00 A.M. to ensure that by 8:00 A.M. they could get in. The room was small and only about twenty-five people could be admitted at a time. At 11:00 A.M. the doors were closed to the public. The people who were still outside had to wait again the following day. The doors were opened again at 3:00 P.M. so that people could get back their passports. Some migrants paid a surrogate to stand in front of the consulate from 4:00 A.M. on, so that they could arrive at 8:00 A.M. and enter without waiting. And anyone who knew an employee of the consulate or who had bribed the policeman at the gate could always get in. People at the back of the line were furious.

In the afternoon a few chairs were placed on the portico of the consulate and an employee called out the names of people whose passports were ready to be returned. Vendors sold candies, ice cream, and cigarettes. Some of the migrants joked about the process, while the policeman at the door kept pushing people away from the employee who was handing out the passports. Some people called out insults; others complained in low voices. This noisy atmosphere sustained the migrants' nervousness. Frustration gave way to joy, however, for those whose passports were returned with the precious U.S. visa stamped inside.

Final Preparation for Departure

The migrant who has received a visa usually visits relatives and friends to let them know the good news. They may offer money to buy anything needed for the trip. Most migrants buy new clothing and give away things they will not take with them.

Relatives come to ask that they not be forgotten. They may complain about their situation, and tell the migrant what they expect in terms of remittances and responsibility toward the rest of the family. The first item on the migrant's agenda is to send the family the money used to pay for the trip; the second, to pay the passage of other members of the family. Some people cry, "I'll never see you again!" They become more emotional as the day of departure draws near. The migrant, though the hero of the moment, may feel ill at ease as he tries to fill all the various roles he is expected to play. The older folks tell him how to behave in New York: don't get involved in politics and stay away from trouble. Everyone wants to help.

The migrant's suitcase may be full of gifts and letters for people in New York. The travel agent may have told him not to take too many things, to travel light in order to convince immigration officials at Kennedy Airport that he is a tourist (if he has a tourist visa, as the great majority do). Such conflicts between the advice of the travel agent and family obligations make him feel pulled in two directions.

The migrant still has to pass through a few formalities at the airport: secure a boarding pass, check his luggage, buy insurance, be ready to answer any questions Haitian immigration officials may ask. This is the final hurdle. The family gathers around, and someone always cries. On the way to the plane the migrant waves goodbye, perhaps for the last time.

The experience aboard the plane does not help. It is the migrant's first plane trip, and he may refuse the meal offered by the flight attendant in the belief that he will have to pay for it. Safety instructions are delivered in English and sometimes in French, but not in Creole. In any case, he is too emotional to pay attention.

At Kennedy Airport, he may ask another Haitian met on the plane to help him in the confusion of the baggage carousel. In this hectic situation, he still has to face U.S. immigration and customs officials. He may make it if his passport has his name on it, if the picture is his, if he has enough money to show, if he has no contraband, and if he does not make the mistake of saying that he is not a tourist. He has been prepared to answer all these questions, but now with all the tension he may go astray.

If someone has come to meet him at the airport, he will feel more or less at ease while they ride together to the friend's or relative's apartment. If no one shows up, he has plenty of addresses in his pocket and will take a taxi. A few New York Haitian taxi drivers are always waiting for easy prey at Kennedy Airport, often taking an indirect route to increase the fare.

Political Space and Emigration

This inquiry into the ecological context of Haitian emigration reveals indirectly the fragility of the migrant's economic base and the cancerous penetration of national-level politics in the matrix of the private sector. Neither structural poverty nor the interplay between politics and emigration is a new phenomenon in Haiti, but the latter has taken on a new symbolic meaning during the two Duvalier administrations. Emigration has become a physical and symbolic escape from a political space that leaves no room for public dissent.

Since the beginning of this century, underground agents have helped Haitian workers to emigrate to Cuba—especially before the Castro revolution—and to the cane fields of the Dominican Republic. In all of these transactions, the hand of the politician has operated behind the scenes.[9] What was an underground activity with its own risks under previous administrations has now received the unofficial stamp of the government and has become one more ingredient in the stew of Haitian politics.

In the present Haitian political situation, the travel agent must be on good terms with various government officials in order to succeed; his business will survive and grow to the extent that it is perceived as an extension of the services provided by the government to its citizenry. The agent must bribe officials in key government positions so that he may easily secure documents on behalf of his clients, for his own political protection, and to be able to compete with other agents; for the possibility that he could be denounced as one who helps enemies of the government to leave the country, and who interacts through his business with exile groups abroad, is always there. Without protection from legitimate officials of the government, the consequences of such a denunciation could be devastating for the agent.

The political structure permeates every aspect of Haitian society. In the context of the presidency for life, where it is difficult to make an overt protest, massive emigration becomes a symbolic form of resistance. Even the simple act of emigration carries a political meaning because of the migrant's dependence on the travel agent, who is himself dependent on government officials who require bribes in order to process the necessary papers. This political meaning of the act of emigration must be taken into account. Insofar as it enters into the migrant's self-image and his conception of the act he is undertaking, it inevitably has an effect on his willingness to tolerate inefficiency and maltreatment by officials.

9. For an example of this kind of corruption during the U.S. occupation of Haiti, see U.S. Congress, House, 1922.

Under the present autocratic regime, there is very little room for the public expression of political dissent and opposition. The political space is totally controlled by the government through coercion, domination, intimidation, and repression. Economic underdevelopment, then, is compounded by political repression to make emigration the best alternative for all who wish to improve their plight.[10]

10. For recent studies on Haitian emigration to the United States, see Laguerre 1980a, 1981, 1982b.

[3]

The Setting: Brooklyn, Manhattan, and Queens

Haitian immigrants arriving in New York City find a landscape that has been largely designed over the years by the practice of residential racial segregation. They must join a black or racially mixed neighborhood. It is from this human ecology perspective that one must analyze the relationships between ethnicity and space as they affect the development of Haitian neighborhoods in New York City.

Patterns of residential racial segregation in New York City have evolved mainly as the result of discrimination against black immigrants from the Deep South and the Caribbean islands. Like the earliest European immigrants, the newcomers were forced to occupy the lowest status positions in the urban social structure and to settle in the poorest districts of the city.[1] European immigrants, however, were able to move out as their economic situation improved and to assimilate with the broader American society; the black immigrants have been denied the opportunity to live elsewhere (Taeuber and Taeuber 1964, 1965; see also Kerner Commission 1972:230).

The allocation of space in New York City is a form of spatial domination whereby racial minority groups are encapsulated in districts that help to reinforce their dependence on the wider society. At the same time, the ghettoization of these ethnic groups

1. Several studies compare the flight of blacks to the urban North with the plight of European immigrants in the United States; see, for example, Kristol 1972, Roucek and Brown 1939, Blauner 1972, Glazer and Moynihan 1970.

provides a niche for the development of their cultural heritage and their integration in American society. Ghettoization does not necessarily mean class homogenization; in fact, the territorial space occupied by the immigrants is more or less divided along class lines that are determined by their previous class positions in the Haitian political economy and the length of time they have lived in New York.

Haitian Neighborhoods

Although Haitian immigrants are scattered throughout the city, the majority are concentrated in the boroughs of Brooklyn, Manhattan, and Queens. A continual flow of Haitian immigrants into these boroughs has resulted in the formation of distinct Haitian neighborhoods. Their distinctiveness is partly the result of adaptive strategies developed by the people who live in these districts, run businesses that attract a Haitian clientele, and participate in local politics, thereby making their presence felt by the larger community.[2] Through the formation of these niches, they have been able to maintain some of their Haitian cultural heritage and to continue their family traditions without feeling immersed in a totally foreign social environment. The adaptation of these metropolitan immigrants to the American way of life depends in part on their ability to create Haitian enclaves within the ecology of New York City.

Brooklyn

An analysis of the 1970 census tracts indicates that Haitian immigrants in Brooklyn have settled primarily in Crown Heights, Brownsville, Park Slope, Flatbush, East New York, and Bedford-Stuyvesant (see Map I). Their neighbors are lower- and middle-

2. The yearly edition of the *Haitian Directory*, published by Henry de Delva, gives an accurate idea of the scope of Haitian businesses in New York. This directory, which provides information on the location and specialties of Haitian-American-owned stores, restaurants, garages, and the like, becomes bigger year by year.

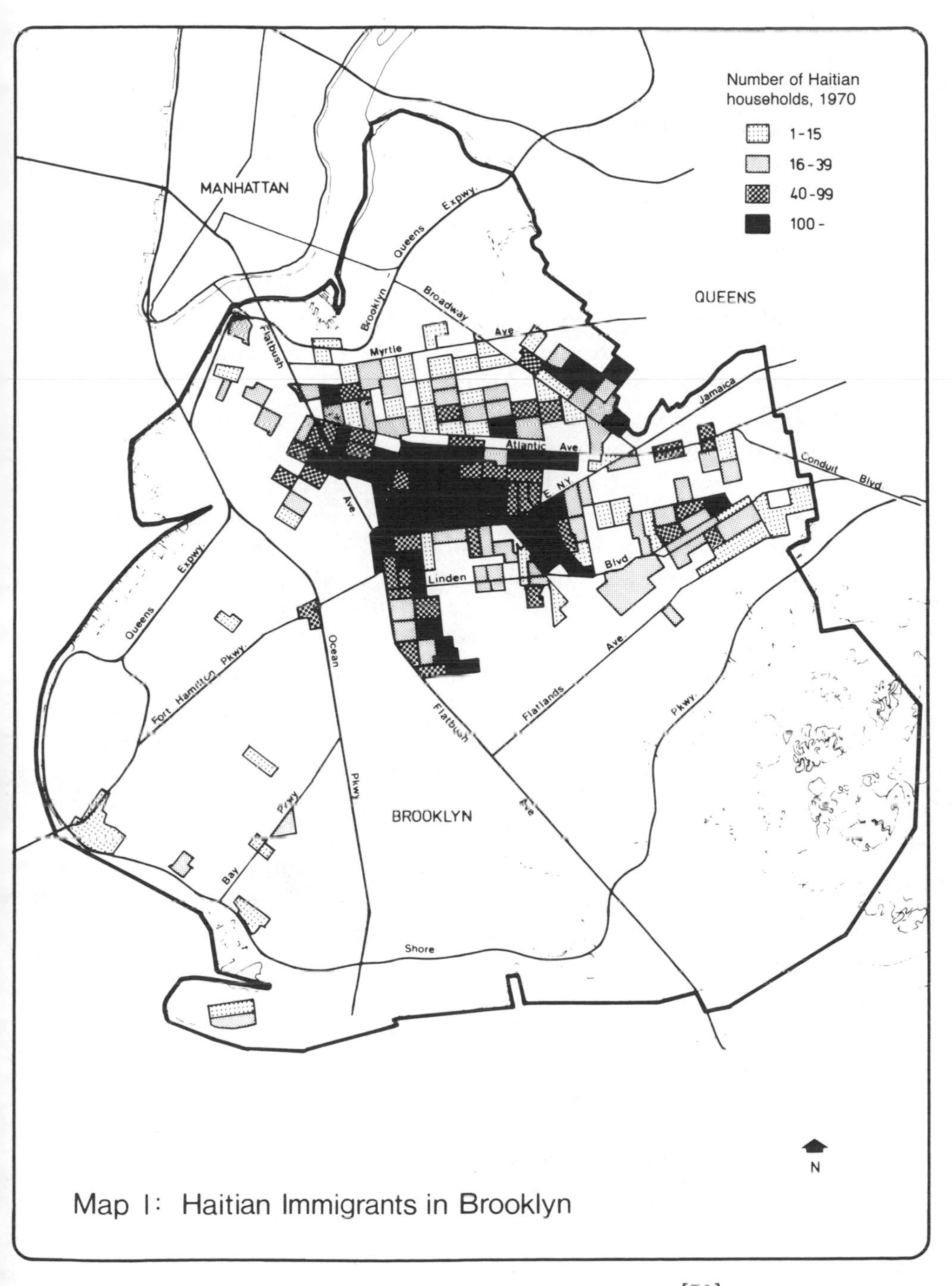

Map I: Haitian Immigrants in Brooklyn

class black Americans, West Indians, Hasidic Jews, Italians, and Puerto Ricans and other Spanish-speaking residents. Members of these ethnic groups maintain daily contact with the Brooklyn Haitians by living in the same buildings, attending the same block association meetings, using the same laundromats, and accompanying their children to the same playgrounds and parks.

Depending on the area, the Brooklyn Haitians live in brick tenements, two-family houses, or high-rise apartment buildings, often within walking distance of a Catholic church and a subway station. Haitians who live in slum tenements often suffer from a filthy environment caused by a dense population of rats and mice. They also often suffer from severe cold in the winter because the landlords do not always provide the necessary heat. In buildings located in crime-ridden areas, Haitians worry about the kinds of friends their children are likely to make. The doors of their apartments are always triple-locked and the residents constantly feel threatened by the possibility of burglary.

In many Brooklyn buildings, all the residents are Haitians. These buildings either are owned by Haitians or have Haitian superintendents. Haitians in search of an apartment often inquire about such buildings among friends or members of the church to which they belong. Haitians are always alert to inform their pastors and friends when there are openings in their buildings, and most Haitian immigrants in Brooklyn find their apartments through word of mouth. Elena Padilla has made a similar observation in a study of the Puerto Rican community in New York City (1958:7). Most of the apartments rented by Haitian-Americans are small, and some are shared with relatives and friends newly arrived from Haiti. Sometimes an older relative is brought to the apartment to take care of young children while the parents work.

Brooklyn residents have access to many hospitals, such as the State University of New York Downstate Medical Center, Kings County Hospital, Brooklyn State Hospital, and the Jewish Hospital for Chronic Diseases. Some Haitians use the services of Haitian physicians in private practice.

Public transportation is widely used by Haitian immigrants. The Brooklyn residents have access, indirectly or directly, to all the trains that cross the city on the IRT (Interboro Rapid Transit), the BMT (Brooklyn-Manhattan Transit), and the IND (Independent) lines. They also use the various buses that crisscross the streets of Brooklyn. When buses and trains cannot be used, they sometimes take taxis, often operated by Haitian cab drivers. Some of these drivers have full-time jobs elsewhere and drive taxis at off-hours.

Catholic churches that serve the Haitian population in Brooklyn include those located on Sterling Place, Kingston Avenue, Linden Boulevard, Church Avenue, Carroll Street, Hancock Street, Eastern Parkway, and 6th Avenue. All of these churches are located in Haitian neighborhoods, and some have Creole- or French-speaking priests on their staffs. Sunday mass is also celebrated in both French and Creole at the Haitian Neighborhood Service Center on Remsen Street.[3]

Manhattan

In Manhattan, Haitian immigrants reside on the Upper West Side from about 69th Street north to 112th Street between Columbus Avenue and Broadway, and from 125th Street to about 168th (see Map II). The social environment on the Upper West Side is not homogeneous. The area has high-rise cooperative apartments, brownstone buildings three stories high, and welfare hotels. In the 1970s Hispanics (Dominicans, Cubans, and Puerto Ricans), black Americans, and Haitians constituted the main ethnic groups of this neighborhood. The area has a large number of restaurants and stores owned by Puerto Ricans and Dominicans. Closer to Columbia University the neighborhood is predominantly white, while from 125th Street northwest it is predominantly black.

Along Amsterdam Avenue two restaurants, a bookstore, a record shop, a money exchange service, and a social club are owned by Haitian businessmen. Here young men "hang out" to take a break from their daily routine. Padilla has found a similar pattern of recreational use of retail establishments in the Puerto Rican community (1958:4). Another Haitian neighborhood service center is located on Amsterdam Avenue.[4] The two Catholic churches

3. This center is sponsored, financed, and operated by the Diocese of Brooklyn. It helps in the resettlement of Haitian immigrants.

4. This center, the oldest in the city, is financed by the State of New York.

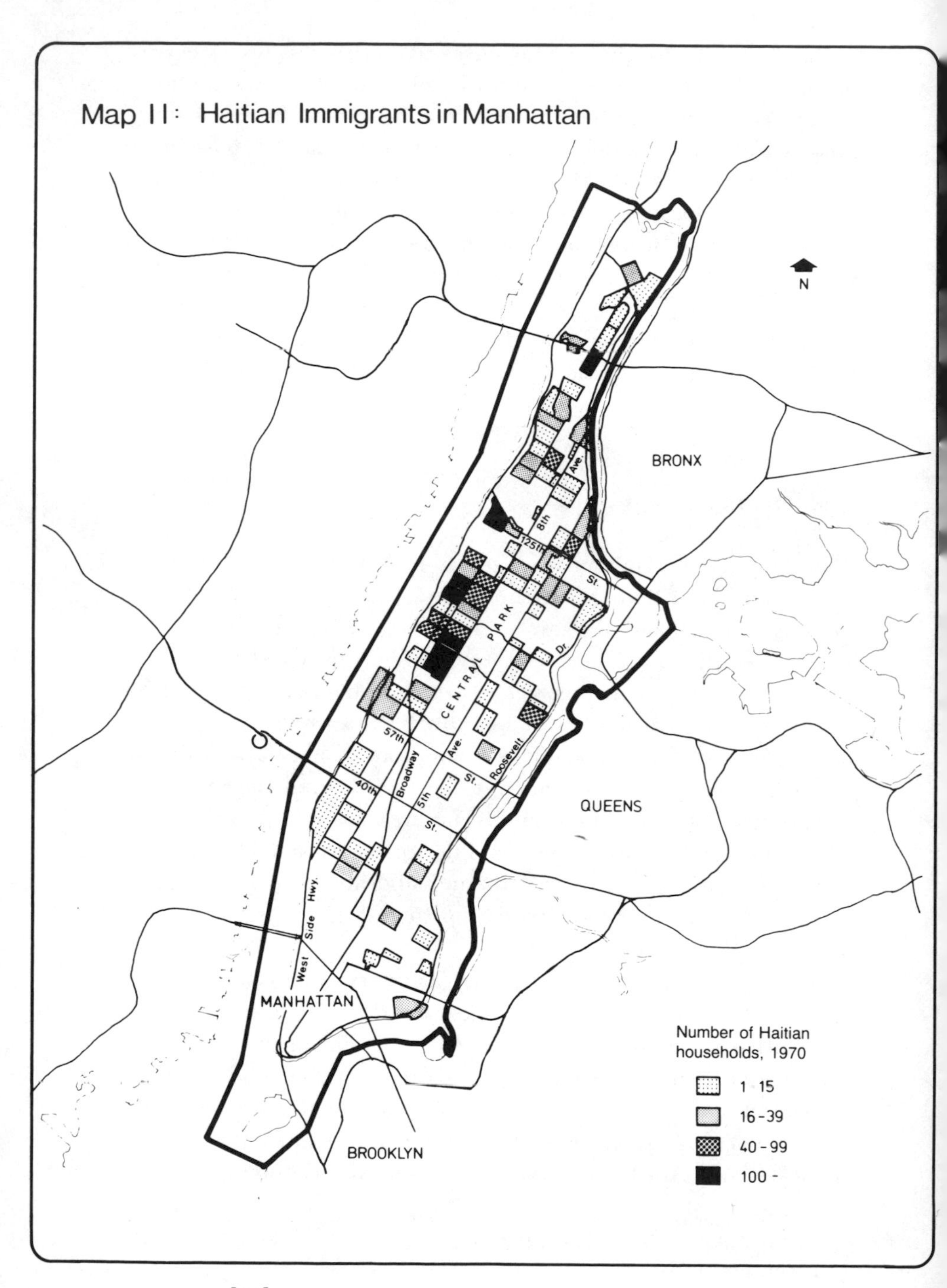
Map II: Haitian Immigrants in Manhattan
N
BRONX
QUEENS
MANHATTAN
BROOKLYN
125th
St.
8th
Ave.
CENTRAL PARK
Dr.
Roosevelt
57th
St.
40th
St.
Broadway
5th
Ave.
West Side Hwy.
Number of Haitian households, 1970
1-15
16-39
40-99
100-

serving the Haitian community are on 82nd Street and 90th Street.

Around the nearby schools, students congregate after class in ethnic groups. Among Haitian students, Creole is used more often than French. Haitian parents who accompany their children to and from school linger to chat and exchange views on the political situation at home or New York social conditions.

The Haitian presence is felt in most of the Upper West Side's public places. Haitians work in schools, health clinics, churches, playgrounds, and parks. Instruction booklets are frequently published in English, Spanish, and French.

Queens

Haitian immigrants live in large numbers in the Queens sections of Corona, East Elmhurst, Queens Village, Cambria Heights, South Jamaica, and Jackson Heights (see Map III). Although many Brooklyn Haitians would prefer to live in Queens, it is an exaggeration to contend that "the poor Haitians in Manhattan and Brooklyn are all yearning to get to Queens" (J. Anderson 1975:2). Haitians are attracted to Queens because of the suburban atmosphere of some of its districts.[5] Living in single-family houses, they feel more secure and less exposed to the muggings that are common in such crime- and drug-ridden areas as Bedford-Stuyvesant in Brooklyn.

Entertainment

Various Haitian-owned night clubs in Queens attract Haitians from all the other boroughs, especially on Saturday nights. Queens can be considered the capital of Haitian entertainment in New York. The night clubs there are believed to be safer than the

5. Queens provides a haven for light-skinned immigrants who used to belong to the old Haitian bourgeoisie. Many former Pétionville residents may be found here. Most of the Haitians in Queens moved there from Brooklyn or Manhattan when they were able to buy their own homes. Haitian-Americans purchase the tropical foods they seek on Linden Boulevard, in grocery stores owned by Spanish-speaking and West Indian immigrants.

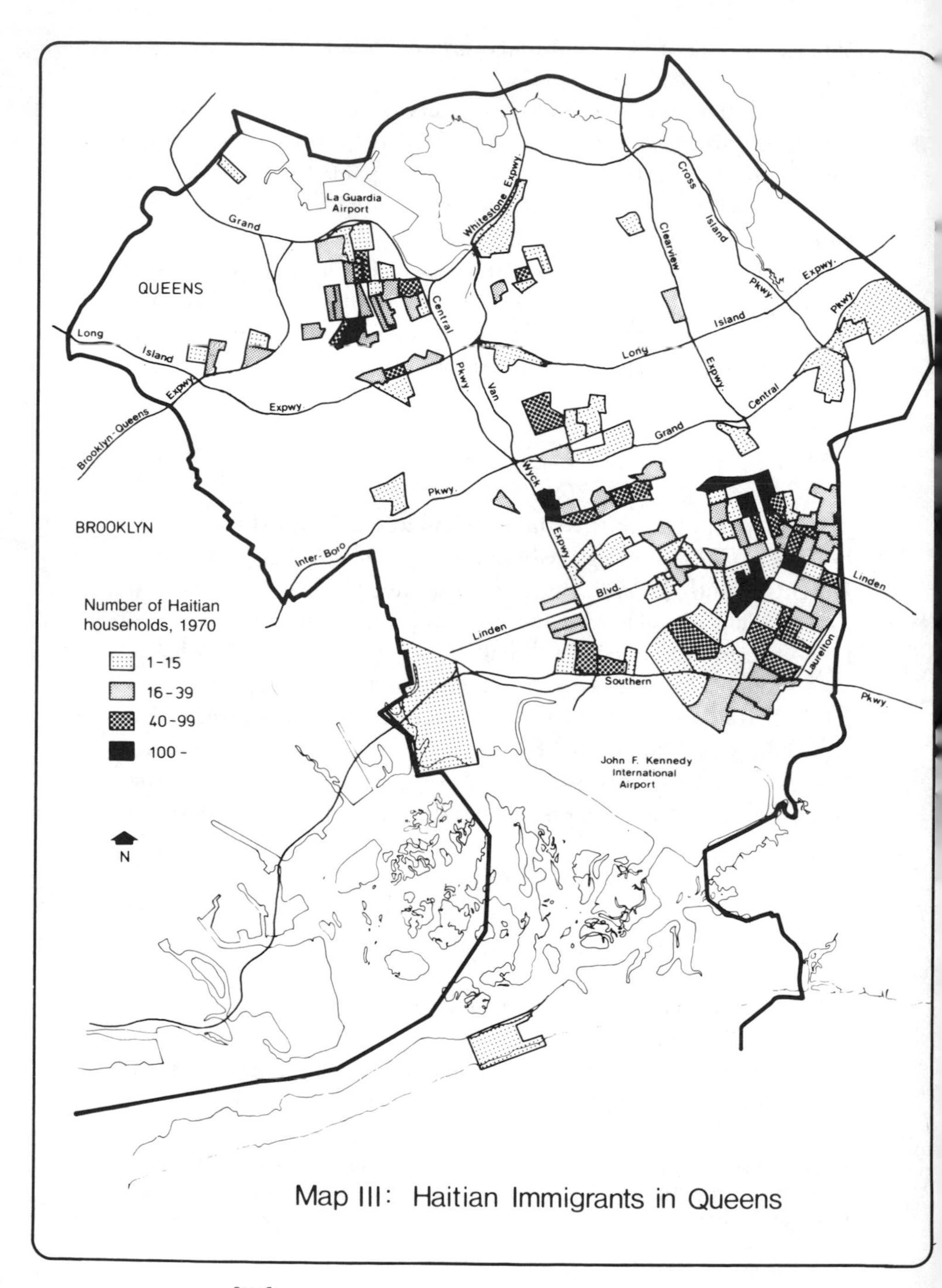

Map III: Haitian Immigrants in Queens

ones in Brooklyn. Young Haitians frequent these places to socialize with fellow countrymen and to seek future spouses.

Soccer games in Queens and in Brooklyn also attract a large number of Haitians. Since the early 1960s, Haitians have been playing soccer during the summertime in school playgrounds and in parks. Over the years, Haitian immigrants have run soccer championship games. On Sunday afternoons many Haitians come to applaud and encourage the Haitian teams. Haitian soccer teams play against Latin American and American teams as well as against each other.

The entertainment that the immigrants enjoy most is the Saturday-evening dances, both private and public. At private parties, friends join with members of the extended family to celebrate baptisms, birthdays, wedding anniversaries, and graduations. I found that most of the people who attended such parties to which I was invited had known each other before they came to New York. Sometimes the majority of guests, as well as the host family, come from the same village or city in Haiti (see also Clérismé 1975).

Public dances held on Saturday evenings in church basements and in Haitian-owned night clubs bring together a cross-section of the population. In the late 1960s, Haitian priests in Brooklyn organized dances in church basements for their parishioners. The people were charged small entry fees, and the money collected was used to pay for electricity and the musicians' services. With the appearance of several jazz bands in the 1970s, most such dances were transferred to Haitian-owned night clubs. Such bands as Tabou-Combo, Shleu-Shleu, Last Stop, Djet X, Delta Express, and Skah-Shah provide Saturday-evening entertainment for the community.

Such community theater groups as Troupe Kouidor and Troupe Djoumba and such Haitian folkloric groups as the Ibo Dancers, the Léon Destiné Dance Foundation, and the Ayida Dance Group concentrate much of their activities during the summer season. Members of the Haitian-American community theater groups are very politicized. Most of their plays, presented in Creole, deal with the oppressive political situation in Haiti and antagonistic black-mulatto relationships. Here, they say in effect, may be found the roots of the present economic mess in Haiti.

In their spare time, men play cards and dominoes. Barbershops and restaurants provide the setting for such nonbetting games. A good deal of Haitians' leisure time is spent in entertaining relatives, friends, and neighbors in their apartments. During such visits immigrants usually talk of the political situation in Haiti, of the parents to whom they still send remittances, and of their own problems in New York.

Religious Establishments

The Catholic church has done much to alleviate the burden of large numbers of Haitian immigrants. Through the church, they continue ritual practices to which they were accustomed in Haiti. Baptisms, weddings, and funerals and the weekly Sunday mass bring segments of the community together. These gatherings serve as a means of reaffirming the existence of the group as an ethnic entity. The Catholic church plays, indeed, a vital role in the community.

Before 1966, Haitians attended Sunday mass in parishes administered by English- and Spanish-speaking priests. As many of them did not understand the priest's language, they acquired no sense of their own emerging ethnic community. During the summer of 1966, however, a Haitian priest, Father Rodrigue Auguste, arrived from Canada to visit relatives and friends in New York, and was invited to join the parish of St. Teresa in Brooklyn to minister to the growing Catholic Haitian population there. He founded the Organisation Chrétienne de la Communauté Haïtienne (Christian Organization of the Haitian Community) and became the first Haitian priest to work among Haitian immigrants in New York.

According to the annual report issued in 1976 by Father Guy Sansaricq, the executive director of the Queens-based Haitian Apostolate Office, Brooklyn, Manhattan, and Queens then had eight Haitian priests and two French priests who were formerly missionaries in Haiti (Sansaricq 1978). They coordinated weekly Bible study groups, sacrament preparation classes, and evening adult education classes in English, in addition to their regular priestly duties. In 1975 they published a Creole hymnbook, which they now use during Sunday services. They have also published a quarterly, *Sel*, which carries articles in both French and Creole on subjects of concern to the community. Their most visible effort has been their continuing success in securing financial support and legal assistance, with the help of the World Council of Churches, for the Haitian refugees in Miami.

The Catholic church has also given financial support to the Haitian Neighborhood Service Center in Brooklyn. "The Center . . . has a staff of about six employees that work full time and assist the immigrants with their problems in education, evening schools, job training, employment, immigration and social agencies. Youth and senior citizen activities are also provided" (Sansaricq 1979:24).

A few Protestant churches—Baptist, Episcopal, Seventh-Day Adventist, Pentecostal—have Haitian ministers. The migration of some Haitian Protestants has been facilitated by their former pastors in Haiti. In the 1960s several American Protestant missionaries established churches in Haiti, and have succeeded in securing job affidavits for would-be migrants among their parishioners. Haitian Protestants in New York get much economic, spiritual, and emotional support from their brethren. Protestants are very active in helping each other, especially in times of crisis. They care for the old and the needy, make home visits, and pray for the sick.

Some Protestant churches attract people who have known each other in Haiti. People hold membership in some churches because they knew the pastor in Haiti. Protestant churches organize picnics for their members, giving them the opportunity to meet each other and to socialize. They serve also as placement services for people in search of jobs and apartments to rent. Their "necessity fund" is used to care for the needy, to assist newly arrived immigrants, and to help their parent churches in Haiti.

Although voodoo is widely practiced among Haitians in New York, a voodoo temple has yet to be built in the city (Cassidy and Wakin 1978). The voodoo places I have visited are single rooms in basements and apartments.

On June 24, 1978, I attended a voodoo ceremony in Brooklyn which was organized by one of my informants for the purpose of communicating with her spirit protector, Ogou Féraille. She had been sick and had telephoned a voodoo priest in Haiti to learn the cause of her illness and the appropriate course of action. The priest had advised her to hold a ritual of thanksgiving for her spirit protector.

The ceremony began at exactly 9:00 P.M. in the consultation room of a priest's apartment. The priest, accompanied by two assistants, my informant, and her family, stood in front of a small altar laden with chromolithographs of Catholic saints, a crucifix, an *ason* (ritual rattle), a few candles, a flag, some flowers, and ornate bottles containing voodoo medicine. Other relatives, friends, and guests conversed in the living room and kitchen.

There was no drumming, as in a typical voodoo ceremony in Haiti, but simply singing with clapping of hands. With his *ason*, the priest invited all the participants to sing and dance as a way of welcoming the spirits who were traveling from abroad to visit with them. When this first phase of the ritual was completed, the priest drew signs (*vèvè*) on the floor of the consultation room while food and drink were served to the guests.

After a brief pause, the priest proceeded with the ritual of possession. While he was dancing with my informant, he became possessed by Ogou Féraille. The spirit revealed that the informant's illness was caused by her neglect of her ritual duties. She was told that she would soon be well again, and that she would not forget to hold a ceremony every year in honor of her spirit protector. After the possession ritual, everyone continued to sing, dance, eat, and drink in an atmosphere of contagious happiness for several hours.

Voodoo gatherings are held periodically in New York and voodoo ceremonies are performed on the eve of the celebration of the feast of some Catholic saints, such as St. James and St. John. The feast of the Magi is widely celebrated by voodooists in New York. During November, voodooists are possessed by *guédés*, spirits of the dead in voodoo mythology.

Voodoo priests may be either male or female. In New York they serve as cult leaders, folk psychiatrists, and healers. They may have full-time jobs and see their followers on weekends. Each priest maintains a voodoo room in which to receive clients who believe that spirits are bothering them. This is a one-to-one consultation. In curing and healing sessions, as well, only the priest and the client are involved. Curing séances are kept secret because clients are likely to be undocumented immigrants who are unwilling to go to hospitals.

The Schools

Haitian students are enrolled in both public and parochial schools in the city. Haitian families try hard to send their children to school in order to provide them with a means of upward mobility in American society. The children, however, have tremendous problems in adapting themselves to the New York school system.[6]

Undocumented aliens who are obliged to work two low-paying jobs have very little time to socialize with their children. Even households with legal immigrant status usually contain no one who can help children with their homework. Apartments are small and crowded. The constant coming and going of other people make it difficult for students to concentrate on their studies. Often they know more English than their parents, and the elder must depend on the younger for translation.

The possibility of getting transcripts from Haiti is often slim. This is a very serious problem when Haitian students try to matriculate in New York schools (Seligman 1977). Students who attended St. Martial College in Port-au-Prince, for example, cannot get their records because the Holy Ghost Fathers who used to run the secondary school were expelled from Haiti by François Duvalier. It is also difficult to obtain a copy of one's baccalaureate diploma from Haiti because the files of the Board of Education are carelessly kept.

The adaptation of Haitian children to the American school system is difficult because they are accustomed to a different method of learning (Laguerre 1979c). In Haiti the emphasis is on memorization; students are asked to memorize several pages of essays

6. For a general statement and commentaries on the language situation among Haitian immigrants in New York, see Buchanan 1979b, Adriyin 1973, and Y. Déjean 1977. For a discussion on the language problem of Haitian immigrants in Quebec, see Soler 1980.

each day in the French language, essays that they do not always understand. In the United States the emphasis is on comprehension.

Most Haitian children are forced to enroll in ghetto schools, where teachers' performance often leaves something to be desired and where Haitian students are harassed by other children. Because of the language handicap, they become shy and reluctant to socialize with students of other ethnic groups. Instead they socialize among themselves in school playgrounds and alleys.

The language problem looms large for Haitian immigrant students. The language used in the classroom is not the one spoken at home, and students must constantly switch from one to the other. This situation does not help them to compete with other students who do not have so severe a language handicap. The New York Board of Education is developing and implementing a program of bilingual and bicultural education for students whose mother tongue is not English. This program is provided to any elementary school in the city where at least twenty students speak the same foreign language. Six school districts in Brooklyn, Manhattan, and Queens provide bilingual programs to French- and Creole-speaking Haitians. In 1977 about 1,700 Haitian elementary school children were enrolled in such bilingual programs. The Board of Education also has bilingual programs in Wingate, Prospect, Southshore, Brandeis, and John Jay high schools, and one in the High School Equivalency Program. About 3,000 Haitian high school students were enrolled in the program in 1977 (Laguerre 1979a:18).

In general, Haitian students are polite, hard workers and very proud. A sociologist who worked with Haitian high school students in Boston wrote that "they want to learn, they never go to sleep in class the way the other students do. Toward the end of the school year they are the only students on whose daily presence the teachers can count" (Verdet 1976:232). This pattern of behavior is influenced by the fact that Haitian parents perceive education as a way of improving the socioeconomic condition of their children. Thus the students receive much encouragement from their parents and the community to pursue professional careers. It is likely that in the years ahead many of them will go to college.

Voluntary Associations

Voluntary associations, created to meet the specific needs of immigrants, play an important role in easing their adaptation to their new environments (see Little 1965). Oscar Handlin has found that in nineteenth-century America, "under the pressure of their difficult situations, people of common background drew together for the satisfaction of common social and cultural needs" (1959:18). Fraternal and social associations serve as links between the immigrants and the host country, and provide a social context within which cultural traditions can be maintained and progressive adaptation to the new milieu achieved (Bernard 1975:19). Though the various associations tend to have their own specific goals, for many people they highlight the experience of belonging to the same ethnic group.

West Indian immigrants in the United States have participated in numerous voluntary associations. In a study of the West Indian community in Los Angeles, Joyce Bennett Justus (1976:138) has shown that "clubs have become an important means for the preservation of cultural pride and West Indian national identity. They provide a locus of non-familial interaction." The New York Haitian community supports several church-affiliated social and problem-solving voluntary associations. Some attract a large membership; others were created to meet the needs of a specific group of people in the community. Some are oriented toward maintaining cultural links with Haiti; others are geared toward the integration and full participation of the immigrants in American society. Some are economic or political organizations; others strive to meet the spiritual and religious needs of their members.

A few Haitian voluntary associations try to unite immigrants who came from the same villages. La Fraternité Valléenne is one such voluntary association. The goal of these associations is to strengthen the ties of friendship and solidarity among their members and to help finance humanitarian projects in their respective villages. Some associations have financed the construction of schools and hospitals in rural Haiti. They usually send the funds to the parish priest in the village and ask him to oversee any ongoing project there. To collect funds, these associations organize pilgrimages, picnics, and public dances.

Ethnicity and Residential Segregation

As we have seen, the development of Haitian neighborhoods in New York City is closely related to the practice of residential segregation in the United States. In the 1920s most upper-class and educated Haitian immigrants who fled to New York settled in Harlem.[7] The immigrants who came during the Duvalier era represent the whole demographic spectrum of Haitian society. Although they have found a city less strictly segregated, especially the lower- and middle-class neighborhoods, the majority of them still live among other blacks. Racial segregation, however, has not caused the development of homogeneous black neighborhoods. It simply restricts the free movement of racial ethnic groups and confines them to specific quarters. Within the boundaries of the black neighborhoods, ethnic niches are based on social class and national origin. The Haitian situation needs to be understood in this light.

An analysis of the 1970 census tracts, on-site visits, and observations of Haitian community leaders have led me to the conclusion that educated and middle-class Haitian immigrants tend to live in the better and more integrated sections of Brooklyn, Manhattan, and Queens.[8] This class segregation among Haitian immigrants, reflected in the patterns of housing, seems to corroborate earlier findings.[9] In a study of racial segregation in the New York metropolis, Nathan Kantrowitz (1976:37) has shown that "rich blacks are segregated from poor blacks as rich whites are from poor whites" (see also Kantrowitz 1973:80). Therefore it is correct to say that incoming black immigrants from the Caribbean have limited opportunities to choose the black or racially mixed neighborhood

7. Harlem was then considered to be the cultural capital of black America. For an analysis of the evolution of the black population in Harlem, see Osofsky 1963.

8. As early as 1920, Bedford-Stuyvesant had the largest concentration of blacks in Brooklyn; see Scheiner 1965:24. Between 1940 and 1960, the black population in Brooklyn increased tremendously; Rosenwaike 1972 gives the exact figures. It has been estimated that "nearly 40 percent of city blacks made their home in Brooklyn in 1970" (Connolly 1977:135).

9. Racial segregation remains an important variable in the housing pattern of New York, and continues to have a negative impact on the racial attitudes of both blacks and whites. "Every New Yorker carries a computer in his head, and race is probably the prime variable in its equations" (Hacker 1975:128).

that best fits their class interests, aspirations, and ethnic affiliation.

In a major study of residential segregation in American cities, Stanley Lieberson (1963:18) has shown that "the process of assimilation is bound up with the process of residential segregation in American cities." His conclusion certainly holds true in the case of the Haitian-Americans. Within the ecological boundaries of their neighborhoods Haitian immigrants experience the reality of racial oppression, perceive the American reality, interpret the American way of life, and adapt to the constraints of the wider social system.

In such a setting, ethnic identity symbolizes the reality of the immigrants' dependence on the wider society. This identity is either maintained as an instrument of ethnic strengths and used as an adaptive strategy for specific purposes or rejected as a reminder of one's dependence. In any case, the feeling and experience of dependence mark the immigrant's cultural identity in any residentially segregated society.

[4]

Family Organization

The development of Haitian enclaves is made possible through the institution of the family. It is there that a bond with the old country is maintained consciously or unconsciously. It is also there that the adaptation to the new country is carried out. The family provides a niche within which cultural continuity can be adapted to the exigencies of the new environment. Through the medium of the family, which influences the behaviors of its members through the mechanism of socialization, immigrants are able to retain some of their cultural heritage and develop an awareness of their ethnic legacy.

The role of the ethnic family in keeping alive the subjective experience of one's ethnic and cultural heritage has already been spelled out: "The family is particularly important in studying the persistence of ethnicity because of its dual function as the repository of the cultural legacy and as the situs of the process by which that legacy is transmitted from one generation to the next" (McCready 1974:154). In the Haitian-American situation, this legacy is maintained and revitalized through ongoing relationships with kin in Haiti and New York and through the socialization of children in family ways.

The continuing migration of Haitian men and women to the United States has wrought many structural changes in the social organization of the Haitian family.[1] In an earlier study I explained

1. A few studies have dealt with the plight of Haitian immigrants in the United States. With the exception of Rey 1970, Buchanan 1979a, Clérismé 1975, and La-

the impact of emigration on the Haitian family and household organization (Laguerre 1978a). Here my concern is the socioeconomic adaptation of Haitian immigrant families in New York. Since the household is the most important unit for social reproduction, one must study its formation and functioning if one is to understand the adaptation process of the immigrants. The household provides a niche in which traditional values are challenged, behavioral conflicts are intensified, and adaptive strategies are developed.[2] It is within the family that immigrants discuss their perceptions of American values, attitudes, and life styles. In the process new kinds of relationships may develop between husband and wife, parent and child.

Haitian family organization in New York City can be best understood in terms of the household history approach. Each immigrant household has a life history, and the composition of the household at various stages of its life cycle can shed enormous light on its evolution and functioning, and consequently on the adaptation of its members to the host society. My concern here is not to delineate in any mechanical fashion what Meyer Fortes (1958) and Jack Goody (1958) refer to as the "developmental cycle of the domestic group," but rather to focus on the process of the formation of immigrant households and the reunification of families. The recruitment of members into a primal household and the departure of others without its complete dissolution is a dynamic process that is at the very heart of the adaptation of Haitian immigrants to New York City.

During the life history of a household, members establish networks of relationships with relatives and friends, forging bonds that are periodically strengthened by the development of effective adaptive strategies for the survival of the household as a whole. The study of household histories, focusing on the formation and relocation of households, becomes pivotal to an understanding of the process by which Haitian families function in New York.

---

guerre 1978a, none deals in any depth with the socioeconomic adaptation of the Haitian family (see Souffrant 1974, Glick 1975, Schiller 1977, Fontaine 1976).

2. By "adaptive strategy" I mean the various tactics and ways that the immigrants have developed to cope with everyday problems in the United States (see Whitten and Whitten 1972).

Resettlement of an Extended Family

A recurrent theme in the literature on family migration is that the migration of a member is likely to produce a chain migration (MacDonald and MacDonald 1964, Tilly and Brown 1967, Rubin 1960, Graves and Graves 1974).[3] The phenomenon of chain migration is certainly at play in the migration of Haitians to the United States (Laguerre 1980a). Indeed, many informants spoke with sensitivity about their obligation to pay for the passage of other members of the family and their role in welcoming newly arrived friends and family members to New York.

One extended family's resettlement process is discussed here in order to show that it is productive to study Haitian family organization in New York City at four distinct levels: (1) the level of interactions among household members, (2) that of interactions of household members with members of the extended family living in New York, (3) that of interactions of household members with the rest of the extended family still living in Haiti, and (4) that of interactions of household members with friends and neighbors in New York. Josephine's family exhibits this fourfold continuum (see Table 1).

In November 1957, one month after François Duvalier was sworn into office, André, a former detective under the administra-

Table 1. The composition of Josephine's household, 1957–72

	Husband	Wife	Wife's goddaughter	Wife's sister	Wife's nephew	Wife's cousin	Wife's brother-in-law
1957	+	–	–	–	–	–	–
1960	+	+	–	–	–	–	–
1962	+	+	+	–	–	–	–
1963	–	+	+	–	–	–	+
1964	–	+	+	+	–	–	–
1965	–	+	–	+	+	–	–
1966	–	+	–	+	–	–	–
1968	–	+	–	–	–	–	–
1970	–	+	–	–	–	+	–
1972	–	+	–	–	–	+	–

+ = full-time resident; – = absent member.

3. Grace Anderson (1974) has shown how Portuguese migrants use their kinship networks to ensure the success of their relocation in Canada.

tion of Paul-Eugène Magloire, president of Haiti from 1950 to 1956, migrated to New York City. André was originally from Cayes, a major city in the south of Haiti. Although he had moved earlier to Port-au-Prince, most of his relatives still lived in Cayes. In 1957 it was not difficult for a person with vocational training to get a U.S. tourist visa, and André had a vocational diploma. A mechanic, he found employment soon after his arrival in New York. Early in 1960 his wife, Josephine, who had obtained an immigrant visa, joined him. Because she knew very little English, Josephine took work as a domestic. Later, as her English improved, she tried some factory jobs, and eventually she found a permanent position with the Brooklyn post office.

André and Josephine had no children of their own. Josephine, however, had a goddaughter in Haiti, Micheline, whom they considered their fictive daughter. It is common throughout Latin America for a godmother to take moral and economic responsibility in the upbringing of her godchildren (Mintz and Wolf 1950, Laguerre 1978a, Bastien 1951, 1961). Following this tradition, they decided, with Micheline's parents' approval, to bring her to New York City. André was sick from time to time, and Josephine thought that Micheline's presence in the household would make things easier. She could help with household chores, especially when Josephine was at work. Micheline arrived in New York during the summer of 1962. André died a year later. After his death, Josephine continued to send remittances to his relatives until she was able to bring her late husband's youngest brother to New York. Since then, this brother-in-law has been taking care of members of his extended family in Haiti and Josephine no longer feels any economic obligation toward her husband's relatives.

Political events in Haiti accelerated the migration of other members of Josephine's extended family. In 1964 François Duvalier, through the manipulation of the vote, was elected president for life (Diederich and Burt 1964). A few Haitians were preparing to invade the island from New York (Cando and Jorge 1966). Other Haitian rebels were already in an offensive position in the Dominican Republic (Bodson, Ripet, and Lefèvre 1970). Foreign embassies in Port-au-Prince were crowded with people asking for political asylum (Manigat 1965). That same year, the Tontons Macoutes invaded the Dominican embassy in search of terrorists or opponents of the government.[4] Five U.S. warships were posted in the vicinity, ready to intervene, according to reports provided to Duvalier by the Haitian Air Force and the director of the Haitian Intelligence Agency (Duvalier 1969). The international press continually reported political repression on the island, with escalating numbers of people jailed and killed. Under pressure from her parents back home, Josephine agreed to help other members of her family to migrate to New York. She sent first for her sister Danielle.

Danielle lived with Josephine for a year and a half, until her son arrived from Haiti. When Danielle moved out, she helped Josephine pay for the passage of another sister, Jacqueline. Jacqueline arrived in 1966 and spent a year in Josephine's apartment.

With financial aid from her sisters, Josephine then sent for her cousin François. François arrived toward the end of the summer of 1970, and in 1972 he sent for his wife. As both he and his wife have tourist visas, they have not yet been able to send for their seven children, who are now with their maternal grandmother in Port-au-Prince. At the time of this survey (1977), the cousin and his wife were still living with Josephine in Brooklyn. Josephine wants them to stay with her for companionship.

Josephine has played a major role in the migration of members of her family. Her apartment has been used by her sisters, goddaughter, and cousins in the early stages of their resettlement. Their adaptation was eased by Josephine's ability to help them find jobs, basically by introducing them to her networks of contacts. Even today Josephine remains the main node in the complicated network that forms the base of this extended family. Josephine is called upon whenever her sisters, nephews, and nieces are about to make a major decision. Her apartment is like a mother house for her relatives. Everyone feels some obligation toward her.

When she left Josephine's apartment, Danielle and her son Janthy moved to Brooklyn. Her husband, Antonio, and her other children, Marise, Versina, and Joseph, were still in Haiti. Every

4. The Tontons Macoutes, a civilian armed force, were created by François Duvalier to counteract the power of the military. They are known for their brutality and terroristic methods.

two years she sent for one of them, and now they are all living in New York. In addition to her husband, sons, and daughters, Danielle has also welcomed to New York a sister-in-law and two nephews who shared the apartment with her until the sister-in-law was able to find a job (see Table 2).

The three oldest children, Janthy, Marise, and Versina, are now married to Haitians they met in New York. Micheline, Josephine's goddaughter, served as godmother at Versina's wedding. The youngest son, Joseph, has a girl friend in Haiti whom he hopes to marry after he graduates from Brooklyn Community College. Janthy, who is living in Queens, has an M.A. degree and is a leading figure in the family; he is the one on whom members of the extended family rely for help in immigration and business matters.

In January 1965 a Haitian man, Gabriel, saw Micheline's picture in the living room of her parents' home in Port-au-Prince. With the consent of her parents, he wrote to her. Through their correspondence, Micheline and Gabriel fell in love. During the summer Micheline returned home to marry Gabriel, and shortly afterward he joined her in New York. Josephine helped them find an apartment in her neighborhood.

In 1971 Micheline started bringing her relatives to New York. She sent first for her brother and sister. In 1973 she sent her baby daughter to her mother in Haiti. Three years later, when she was about to separate from Gabriel, she sent for her parents and child. Thus, by the time the divorce was in progress, she had all her relatives with her in New York (see Table 3).

When Jacqueline came to New York, she left a husband and

Table 2. The composition of Danielle's household, 1965–75

	Husband	Wife	Children	Wife's sister-in-law	Wife's nephews
1965	–	+	+	–	–
1967	+	+	+	–	–
1968	+	+	+	+	–
1969	+	+	+	+	–
1971	+	+	+	–	–
1972	+	+	+	–	+
1973	+	+	+	–	+
1974	+	+	+	–	+
1975	+	+	+	–	–

+ = full-time resident; – = absent member.

Table 3. The composition of Micheline's household, 1965–77

	Husband	Wife	Wife's sibling	Children	Wife's father	Wife's mother
1965	+	+	–	–	–	–
1968	+	+	–	+	–	–
1971	+	+	+	+	–	–
1973	+	+	+	–	–	–
1976	–	+	+	+	+	+
1977	–	+	+	+	+	+

+ = full-time resident; – = absent member.

Table 4. The composition of Jacqueline's household, 1967–77

	Husband	Wife	Children	Wife's sister-in-law
1967	+	+	–	–
1969	+	+	–	+
1970	+	+	+	–
1971	+	+	–	–
1972	+	+	+	–
1973	+	+	–	–
1974	+	+	+	+
1975	+	+	–	–
1976	+	+	+	–
1977	+	+	–	–

+ = full-time resident; – = absent member.

four children in Haiti. It was ten years before all six of them were together again in Brooklyn (see Table 4). In 1977 Jacqueline and her husband were living in the same building as one of their married children. The other children, who have college degrees, live in Queens.

Household Formation

Haitian households in New York City are formed on the basis of four types of marriage arrangement: *mariag de goudin, mariag bay bous, mariag rézidans,* and *bon mariag*. The *mariag de goudin* is an arrangement by which a Haitian living in the United States marries a lower-class person (a citizen or holder of a resident visa) in order to be eligible for U.S. resident status. The American who enters into such a marriage is likely to be an uneducated factory worker. As one would imagine, such marriages are often sources of cultural conflict for both partners.

The *mariag bay bous* is contracted for the purpose of permanent migration. A Haitian who has U.S. resident status returns to the island, marries a would-be migrant, and brings his or her new spouse to the United States. Sometimes this kind of marriage is arranged by relatives; the couple may not know each other at all. The spouse who has resident status pays for the passage of the other, who now is eligible for a resident visa. This practice is not the monopoly of Haitian immigrants. Joyce Bennett Justus (1976:135) has found that many West Indians in Los Angeles "send money to pay passages for prospective brides or bridegrooms."

The *mariag rézidans* is a marriage between Haitians already living in the United States, one of whom has U.S. resident status while the other does not. The legal resident often comes to believe that the other has entered into the marriage in order to become a resident. It is evident that the question of residence is of some importance in the motivation and arrangements of such marriages. Some students use this device to regularize their status.

A *bon mariag* is any marriage contracted in Haiti before the couple decided to migrate to New York or contracted in the United States by two Haitians who share the same status as immigrants: either both are legal residents or neither is. The aim of the *bon mariag* is to establish a husband-wife union; it is not an arrangement entered into for the purpose of gaining a resident visa.

One partner in a *bon mariag* or a *mariag bay bous* may live alone while waiting for the other to migrate. The first partner to come to New York plays a major role in the socialization of the other. If the wife is the first to migrate, she is likely to continue to run the household after her husband arrives, until he is able to take control of the situation.

Households formed by unmarried people living together or composed of a mother and her children may be of some significance in the Haitian community in New York.[5] These household

5. There is now an abundant literature on Caribbean matrifocality; see, for example, R. T. Smith 1956; Kunstadter 1963; Greenfield 1966; M. G. Smith 1971; Mintz and Davenport, eds., 1961; Bastien 1951, 1961. Melville and Frances Herskovits (1947), among the first anthropologists to explain the occurrence of female-headed households in Afro-America, argue that matrifocality must be understood

forms, however, are not common in Josephine's extended family. In any case, the data we have are not conclusive, and in speaking of family dynamics I do not refer to common-law marriage arrangements or to female-headed households.[6]

Husband and Wife

Whatever the kind of marriage arrangement contracted, the husband-wife relationship, which was asymmetrical in Haiti, often becomes more symmetrical in New York. It is probably in matters related to family that the Haitian community in New York has experienced the most fundamental changes. In the view of an observer, "the old family organization is no longer relevant. The shifting roles, the change of standards, status, personal values, contribute to the breakdown of the Haitian family organization" (Rey 1970:31).

In the first stage of the resettlement process, the role of the head is played by the breadwinner and the partner more experi-

---

as a retention of West African culture in the life styles of the Afro-Caribbean people. Their cultural interpretation of the matrifocality phenomenon contrasted with Franklin Frazier's (1939) sociological interpretation, which explained matrifocality in terms of the marginal economic situation of blacks in the United States. R. T. Smith (1956), who conducted his field research in Guyana, brought more subtleties to the debate by arguing that matrifocality can be a transitional phase in the developmental cycle of the Afro-Caribbean household. Thus he proposes that by looking at household histories, one can reach a better understanding of the complexity of family life in the Caribbean and in Afro-America in general. It is in the works of Carol Stack (1976), Demitri Shimkin et al. (1978), and Herbert Gutman (1976), however, that one becomes aware that the households of the black extended family are interrelated, and that through network analysis one can decipher the various levels of relationships, support mechanisms, familial solidarity, and survival strategies used by individual members to cope with their everyday problems.

6. One of the problems to which Robert Davison (1962:67) alluded in his study of West Indian immigrants in Great Britain was the breakdown of consensual unions in the migration process. The same observation can be made of some Haitian immigrants in the United States. A migrant who has been engaged in a consensual union, which is protected by folk laws in Haiti and thus achieves a certain stability, may find it easier to marry someone else here than to sustain the relationship. Since such a union is not legally recognized in the United States, such a person finds it all but impossible to send for his or her partner. Emigration thus often leads to the breakdown of such unions.

enced in the city, whether husband or wife. The newcomer has much to learn and probably has not found a job yet, and therefore is economically dependent on the partner.

If one spouse has entered the country as a tourist while the other is a legal resident, the task of adjustment to each other may be complicated by ambivalence. The spouse without resident status must rely on the other to sign the immigration papers and to help in other ways. Husbands thus sometimes find themselves dependent on their wives. After such a man acquires a visa, the pattern of the relationship already established may be difficult to change.

A common problem seems to emerge in most of the *mariag bay bous*. The newcomer (let's say the husband) may be asked to bring his paycheck directly home, as he probably does not know English and so is unable to cash it himself, and to conform to the household pattern shaped before his arrival. This first phase may be painful for him. His wife has in all probability been sending money back home, and may have assumed additional obligations on the assumption that she will be able to use her husband's earnings. He also has expectations, however, and has assumed some obligations toward his own kin in Haiti. Part of the couple's adaptation to the city consists in settling this matter and working out their budget together.

Strategies are sometimes devised by the partner who has initiated the *mariag bay bous* in order to ease the adaptation of her spouse. One such strategy consists of preventing the new migrant from making contact with persons outside the partner's network of friends. She may be suspicious and highly concerned about her husband's socialization in New York. She may be afraid that other individuals will *monté tèt li* (influence him and lead him in the wrong direction), and so may try to block other contacts. By unplugging the phone when she is at work, for example, she prevents her husband from talking with others *ap bay zin* (receiving gossip information). This encapsulation is done with the best intentions, in order not to damage their relationship in the early stage of the relocation process in an environment of hardship. Their relationship may already be strained by the newcomer's social obligations. In addition, he is under great obligation to her. She has paid his passage, and during the resettlement process he must depend on her financially. This dependency relationship does not evaporate overnight. In time, however, some kind of balance may be struck.

Life in New York has a tremendous impact on the relations between husband and wife. He is asked to help with household duties, sometimes to cook. This is a new ingredient in Haitian household life. If the couple belongs to the middle class, the wife is probably contributing money to the household for the first time. This new type of household economy causes some rearrangement in the husband-wife relationship.[7] A Haitian woman in New York has this to say about the changing role of the wife in the Haitian-American community:

> In our country, the wife has her head down, because she does not work. She sits, wastes time and gossips. She is forced to live with a man because it is he who gives her food, money, clothes and shoes. Here things have changed. We have the means to help financially with the expenses incurred in the household and with the education of our children. Slavery is over. We bring money to the household, and this gives us the freedom to voice our opinions ("mézi lajan nap poté vini, mézi diol nou"). Those who are unhappy with our new way of life: Take it or leave it. [Piè 1975:15]

Married couples who still have close relatives in Haiti tend to stay together despite their problems. The most important problem lies in their responsibility to bring their relatives to New York. A divorce might jeopardize the relatives' chances of leaving Haiti. The few cases of divorce that appear in the sample occurred among the educated middle class, and neither spouse was in the process of sending for relatives.

Parent and Child

The relationships between parents and children are complicated by their different cultural orientations. They are socialized in two different worlds. Often they are in the United States for different

7. It was not possible to compare my findings with those on Haitian women in France (Bastide et al. 1974, Morin 1974) and in Quebec (P. Déjean 1978, Bernardin-Haldemann 1972). These studies tend to focus not on the lower-class family but on student marriages and marriages among Haitian professionals.

reasons. While the children enjoy being in America and intend to stay, some parents, realistically or not, expect eventually to return to Haiti. They retain the traditional values of their Haitian childhoods. They are still Haitians; their children are Americans.

Most children who are socialized in American culture care very little about Haiti. Because all their friends are in New York, they have no strong emotional ties with the island. As parents and children do not necessarily subscribe to the same values, they do not always understand each other. Much intergenerational conflict results. In the same familial niche, parents and children may develop two different views of the United States—as a place of transit and as a place for permanent residence—which reinforce the misunderstandings between them.

The children born in the United States have learned from their parents, friends, and exiles' newspapers of the poverty and political repression on the island. They bring home American friends while their parents associate mostly with other Haitians. More important, they speak English at home, not Creole, as their parents do. The language difference is often a source of communication problems.[8] Because of their knowledge of English, the children must often be culture brokers for their parents, translating for them and interpreting the wider society to them (see Hendricks 1974, Padilla 1958). A Haitian immigrant says:

> One witnesses significant changes in the behaviors of Haitian youngsters in New York. The authority of parents over their children is losing ground. Really, many times, because the parents cannot speak English, they cannot always discipline their children, who must serve as their interpreters. The parents here consult their children for advice. They are afraid sometimes that their children may leave the apartment for good, as happens in the case of American families. For this reason, the parents become more tolerant in regard to their children. In fact, it is almost every day that one hears parents complaining that Haitian children raised in New York City have bad manners. [Soboul 1975:20]

A father who has sent for his children is likely to expect them to bring him their paychecks when they start working. He feels he

8. Harriet Bloch made a similar observation in her study of Polish immigrant women (1976:8).

has a right to do so, and feels doubly justified if he has rented a larger apartment to accommodate them. He may also demand that children pay the passage of their brothers and sisters. Most children of marriageable age resent these demands. When conflict ensues, the children may feel forced to move out. Such a problem usually does not arise with children born in the United States.

Other Members of the Household

Most Haitian households have included a friend or distant relative at some time during their history. Upon their arrival, immigrant newcomers seek out a family to stay with. Many migrants obtain the address of a friend or relative before they leave the island.

It is not easy for an immigrant to stay with a host family without becoming involved in some of their problems. Too, newcomers tend to behave as if they were still in Haiti. Host families expect newcomers to pay for room and board if they can. When the family asks the newcomer to pay something, say $10 a week, the newcomer translates dollars into gourdes (1 gourde = U.S. 20¢) and protests that 50 gourdes is more than one would pay in similar circumstances in Haiti. In fact, of course, $10 cannot cover all expenses for a week. Alternatively, the newcomer may be asked to pay much more, and may indeed be exploited by the host family. Newcomers tend to trust (*fié moun*) their host families, at least for a short time, but outside friends often persuade them that they are being exploited, and eventually the household may erupt in accusations and counteraccusations.

The arrival of a guest often causes competition for space. Many Haitian apartments have two bedrooms, one for the parents and the other for the children. A guest will be asked to sleep on the sofa in the living room or in the children's room. In Haiti no one would complain, as people spend most of their time outside the home. In New York's climate, however, people spend more time indoors. Haitians become more sophisticated, too, and are more disturbed by such conditions. The conflict over space causes conflict in other areas as well. Everyone, for instance, is aware how often the newcomer opens the refrigerator.

Before newcomers manage to secure employment, they are in the position of guests with little to occupy their time but the television and the telephone. They may be unable to pay for the food that the rest of the household works to buy, but they are under stress and feel compelled to eat. Their hosts may tease them by saying they act like recently released prisoners—they do nothing but eat. Newcomers may take on household tasks while the family members are at work and school, cleaning the house and preparing dinner. A newcomer who gets a job will be asked to pay a share of the rent and other expenses rather than a flat weekly fee. The guest may even pay half of the rent, thereby allowing the family to save some money. Such guests are very much appreciated by the family.

Relations with Kin in New York

Not all members of the extended family interact equally. There are subsets or clusters of members who interact continually with each other. Some are constantly helping others whereas others are active only when they are called upon. One may rely on different relatives for help at different times.

The extended family in New York serves as a base of support for family members who are migrating from Haiti. The newcomers find a home and people waiting to help in their adaptation to the city. The family will take responsibility for them until they find work.

The existence of a network of kin is seen most precisely in the matter of remittances. A member of the extended family in Haiti may receive money from one nuclear family in New York one month, from another the next. The families rotate so that the burden will not be the responsibility of any one nuclear family. Solidarity in the extended family can be seen when members pool their money to buy a home. One may get a loan from a relative rather than from a bank. No receipt is required in such cases, and the borrower will have to pay no interest on the loan.

The telephone plays an important role in maintaining the family network. As soon as one receives news from the island, one calls one's relatives in the city to share the news. They keep each other informed about new developments in the political situation on the island. Family members speak with each other on the phone at least once a week. The women's role of maintaining the network of relationships should not be overlooked (see M. E. Smith 1976). Such religious and secular rituals as funerals, baptisms, weddings, birthday parties, and dances serve to maintain the unity of the group and to strengthen kinship ties.

Within each extended family one individual or nuclear family plays a central role in linking the network together. Such a person may be in a position to help others by reason of age, education, or experience in the city. The most educated and experienced member in the extended family will always be called upon for advice.

Linkages with Kin in Haiti

As we have seen, Haitian families in New York maintain strong relationships with kin in Haiti through remittances and child care. The sending home of money is a common practice among West Indians living in the United States and England (Philpott 1968, Frucht 1968, Manners 1965, Gonzalez 1976:42, Garrison and Weiss 1979:274). The amount of money sent is a function of the current phase of the life cycle of the household.

Most migrants who arrive in New York have agreed to repay the people who lent them money for their passage and to send remittances to the other relatives they left behind. Once the ticket money has been repaid and one's immediate family has been brought to New York, one's obligation to send money home declines. One may agree to pay the passages of others if they will then assume the responsibility of aiding the members of their own families at home.

The remittance situation contributes to Haiti's economy, as the money sent to one's family goes indirectly to the government in the form of foreign exchange (Watson 1976:18). Thus the exile groups, while in opposition to the Duvalier administration, still support it indirectly through the remittances they send home.

The style of remittances depends on the style of resettlement. The first person in a family to come to the United States usually establishes a remittance pattern. When the husband comes first, he may send more money to his relatives than to his wife's relatives even after her arrival. At times this situation creates conflict, especially when the wife starts to work and finds that her money passes through a channel she has not helped to establish. Her parents are not receiving their share. This practice, however, is not common in the Haitian community. When it is found, it occurs during the resettlement period. Thereafter the partner concerned will usually find ways to remedy the situation.[9]

Haitian families keep their ties with relatives in Haiti not only through remittances, but also by sending children back home. A good number of families have sent their children to Haiti. The main reason for this practice seems to be economic, though many parents offer concern for their children's education as an explanation. The Haitian educational system stresses Christian values, they say, and in Haiti their children are able to learn French and Haitian customs. This preference contrasts with Nancy Foner's findings among Jamaicans in London (1978:72–73). Justus (1976:136) has found that few West Indians in Los Angeles "regarded the schools as inferior, yet some had sent children back to the island to school. . . . The main concern here, however, was not so much education per se, but the desire to bring up children as West Indians, with West Indian values."

Sending children back home has its own grammatical rules. The families that follow the practice usually have relatives in Port-au-Prince or in other major cities, where hospitals, schools, and communications facilities are available. Those whose parents live in the countryside and who still want to send their children to Haiti usually persuade their parents to settle in Port-au-Prince. Sending children back home is an economic strategy that enables many families to save money toward a home. One informant said:

> I had to pay fifty dollars for my two children every week to go to a day-care center. Also each month I must send sixty dollars back home to my relatives for their subsistence needs. So three years ago

9. The European immigrant family in industrial America went through a similar process (Golab 1977:2). On the impact of industrialization on the immigrant family, see Greenfield 1961.

> I decided to send the children to Haiti in order to save some money. Now the money I used to pay for the day-care center, I save it to buy myself a nice home in Queens.

Haitian families maintain regular contact with relatives in Haiti by visiting them during winter or summer vacations. Some also return during the carnival period and for relatives' funerals. Still others return for familial voodoo gatherings (Laguerre 1980b). The voodoo believers who cannot return to the island because they do not yet have resident status often help to pay for such ceremonies.

Friends and Neighbors

Haitian families in New York maintain contacts with a network of friends and neighbors. This network constitutes another level of adaptation to the city. The existence of such a network seems to confirm Elizabeth Bott's observation (1971:216) that "the immediate social environment of an urban family consists of a network rather than an organized group." Within the total network of the family, there is always some variation in the positions of the various members, the configuration of individuals involved, the density, and the transactional content of their social relations (see Mitchell, ed., 1969). By "transactional content" I mean "the material and non-material elements which are exchanged between two actors in a particular role relation or situation" (Boissevain 1974: 33; see also Kapferer 1969:212). The family relies on friends and neighbors for a host of services. The members of such a network may be either people they knew in Haiti or new acquaintances.

Friendship networks seem to consist of people in three categories: old friends, neighbors, and people one has met in New York—in the workplace, through participation in church- and school-related activities, and in social clubs and other organizations. The immigrants rely on these people for help at different times and often for different reasons.

Old friends who knew each other in Haiti have a common background, and naturally they tend to maintain their relationship in New York. They reminisce, discuss their problems, and share their new experiences in the city. Such relationships are likely to be "multiplex" or "multi-stranded," to use Max Gluckman's terminology (1962:27). One's neighbor and one's new friend from work, for example, are likely to have known each other in Haiti.

The immigrants are careful to maintain survival contacts with neighbors in their apartment buildings. Haitians generally believe that one should always maintain friendly relations with one's neighbors, because they are close at hand in case of need. In New York it is common for Haitian neighbors to visit each other, take care of each other's children, borrow money and kitchen utensils from each other, and offer help in times of illness. Neighbors play an active role in the day-to-day life of the Haitian immigrant family.

Except in the case of schoolchildren, the family's new friends are likely to be other Haitian immigrants. These new acquaintances broaden the family's network of relationships. The more interaction the family has with other Haitian immigrants, the more the community is able to maintain its cultural tradition, its folklore, the Creole language, and other aspects of social life.

Through these networks of friends and neighbors, strategic information is gathered, new experiences are shared, problems encountered in the city are discussed, relationships are expanded, and the process of adapting to American society is eased until the family can finally begin to feel at home in New York.

Ethnicity and Family Adaptation

The experience of Haitian immigrants in New York has much to tell us about the relationships between ethnicity and family adaptation. The awareness of belonging to an ethnic group is usually experienced within the family. The appreciation of the ethnic food, language, music, and values is first learned in the family, which socializes its younger members, consciously and unconsciously, in its own ethnic tradition.

A typical meal of a middle-class Haitian family in New York consists of some of the following foods: fried plantains, fried pork or goat, chicken or beef marinated in Creole sauce, red beans, eggplant, rice, corn, avocado, watercress, bananas, orange or papaya juice. The family often listens to music during the main meal. Haitian music has evolved as a mixture of African rhythms and European melody informed by both secular and religious inspiration. Haitian musicians in New York provide the community with folkloric music associated with voodoo rituals and other musical forms, such as meringue, inspired by secular aspects of Haitian traditional culture.

It is in the family that one may objectively differentiate one's experience from the ethnic experiences of other individuals and appreciate the strengths and weaknesses of one's ethnic tradition. There, too, one can appreciate the similarities of one's experience with that of one's co-ethnics. The plural experience provided by the family as an ethnic niche is instrumental in the development of the awareness of one's ethnicity. For that reason, as Charles Mindel and Robert Habenstein (1976:6) write, "the maintenance of ethnic identification and solidarity ultimately rests on the ability of the family to socialize its members into the ethnic culture and thus to channel and control, perhaps program, future behavior."

Ethnicity is not an all-encompassing concept that can help one to understand every aspect of the adaptation of the immigrant family. Its usefulness as an analytic device varies with the family's class status. Family behavior is a function of both the social class and the ethnic group to which it belongs. Furthermore, the ethnic family cannot be considered as a monolithic unit; it changes over time in its idiosyncrasies, educational attainment, income structure, and the length of time its members have been in the United States.

The class difference among Haitian-American families is reminiscent of the stratification system in Haitian society. Families of elite background in Haiti continue to speak French at home, while the lower-class immigrants speak only Creole. Even within the same social class, regional and ecological variations persist among Haitian-American families. While the majority of lower-class families practice some voodoo, for example, each family may have its own religious traditions. Variations in eating habits and folk traditions can also be observed among families of the same social class.

Haitian families in the United States follow general and specific lines of adaptation. Because of variations of ethnic expression due to class differences, not all Haitian families reach the same level of integration in American society. Light-skinned Haitians and educated professionals face fewer problems than lower-class immigrants in their efforts to become assimilated in American society.

Class membership alone, however, cannot explain the complexity of behavioral patterns of immigrant families. In analyzing the experience of European immigrants in the United States in the second half of the nineteenth century, Richard Ehrlich (1977:ix) found that "behavioral patterns defined in the New World can be explained only with reference to the specific experience of different groups in the old." It is a fallacy, he implies, that European immigrants became culturally assimilated into mainstream American culture. What he says about European immigrants can also be said of Haitian immigrants. They have developed a subculture distinct from mainstream American culture. Ehrlich's analysis corroborates a point made earlier by Milton Gordon (1964) to the effect that structural assimilation does not necessarily lead to cultural assimilation.

The Haitian family is in a continuing process of adaptation to mainstream American society and culture. Whatever its tribulations may be, it provides a context in which one can develop an awareness of one's ethnic background. For it is through the institution of the family that a major part of the ethnic heritage is maintained and transmitted from one generation to the next.

The Functioning of the Immigrant Family

The Haitian family clearly plays an important role in the integration of the immigrants in American society and in the development of a Haitian subculture in New York City. Throughout the migration and resettlement process, the Haitian family maintains its strengths by providing financial support for those left behind, by welcoming new members to the city, and by serving as a support mechanism for the psychological, cultural, and economic adaptation of all persons involved. This analysis of family organization among Haitian immigrants in New York has made possible the following observations.

By and large, Haitians do not emigrate to the United States in family groupings. The lengthy process of getting a U.S. visa and the large amount of money needed to pay a travel agent to procure the proper papers have hindered those who would like to emigrate to the United States legally. This situation may explain why the immigrants go singly through the process.

The migration of a member of an extended family to New York is likely to produce a chain migration. Once here, the migrant often sends for other members of the family. It may be several years before the entire family is able to be together in New York.

Because of the moral responsibility to send for one's relatives and the high cost, by Haitian standards, of travel to New York, immigrants are likely to be economically drained during the first years of their stay in the United States. Much of their financial gain goes to repay the money they have borrowed, to secure U.S. visas for their relatives, and to welcome them to the city.

The Haitian household in New York is used as a stepping-stone for newly arrived members of the family. Here newcomers find a home, and here they receive their early socialization in American society. Further, it is through the older immigrants that they find their way in the city and seek employment.

The socialization of immigrants to mainstream American culture, values, and attitudes develops much faster in schoolchildren than in their parents. Parent-child relationships are modified in New York, where the parents must depend on their children to serve as intermediaries between themselves and the wider society. At times this situation creates intergenerational conflict as the Haitian value system in which the parents have been socialized clashes with the American value system in which the children are being socialized at school.

Haitian women tend to become more assertive in New York, not only because of their economic independence but also because they are immersed in a more pluralistic environment. Husbands tend to be more willing to share household chores with their wives. Consequently, the imbalance in the traditional roles of husband and wife tends to diminish.

The Haitian family maintains a network of kin, friends, and neighbors which allows its members to reach out for support in moments of need. This network consists of a very complex set of relationships, which grows through the recruitment of new friends in such a way that all individuals involved may benefit.

The extended family continues to provide support to its members, serves as a mechanism in the adaptation of newly arrived relatives to the city, and by so doing helps alleviate their psychological stress and tension. It maintains its unity through cyclical gatherings and the leadership role of one of its pioneers. The Haitian family in New York maintains cultural traditions while providing a framework for socialization in American society.

The family is the repository of the Haitian cultural heritage. There the ethnic tradition is kept alive for the children and the community. It serves as a link with the old country, becomes the transmitter of the premigration cultural heritage, and contributes immensely to the survival of the ethnic tradition (see also Hareven 1977:49).

[5]

Earning, Investing, and Saving

The most adaptive strategies for survival are played out in the economic sphere of the Haitian-American community. One such strategy is the manipulation of ethnicity. As William McCready puts it (1976:24), "ethnicity is one of the several identities that people use to position themselves in the social system." Ethnicity is not only an abstract concept used to define and geographically confine an ethnic community, it is also an experience. As an experience, it has a situational context. Manipulation of ethnicity consists of a conscious act to use one's ethnic origin in interactions with people of the same or different cultural background in an effort to gain some benefit from the encounter. In transactional negotiations ethnicity is often used consciously and tactfully.

In the economic sphere, class status and generation of migration are key factors in the adaptation of Haitian immigrants. It was found, for example, that people who held an upper-class position in Haiti have struggled forcefully to achieve upward mobility in the American political economy. Some of those who held a lower-class position have also been able to achieve upward mobility once they came to understand the New York job market. The manifestation of Haitian-American ethnicity reflects underlying economic factors that are indicators of the immigrant's class status and living experience in the United States.

Finding a Job

Ethnicity is one of the strategies that Haitian-Americans use and manipulate in their search for employment. A few underlying principles help explain the ways in which Haitian-Americans secure stepping-stone and permanent jobs. The job-hunting process, the behaviors of workers in the workplace, and the kinds of employment they are most often able to secure are all important factors that need to be explained and delineated. Such a procedure will help us to understand how Haitian immigrants devise strategies to enable them to participate in the nation's mainstream and underground economies.

Not all Haitian immigrants in New York are eligible for all job categories. A number of factors may restrict their access to certain jobs. One such factor is the immigrant's legal status: permanent resident, citizen, or tourist or student not legally eligible for employment. Immigrants without resident status, regardless of skills and education, are barred from white-collar jobs. The only jobs to which they have access are those in which they can be paid "under the table" (dishwashers in restaurants, domestics, and the like) and in factories where they are not asked to show proof of resident status. I estimate that more than one-third of the Haitian-American population falls in this category. They are underpaid and live under severe emotional stress because of the insecurity of their illegal status in the United States. They are in constant fear of being identified by immigration officers, of being denounced by fellow workers and deported. Their fear prevents them from using hospital facilities when they are sick and from calling the police when they are victims of a crime. Most Haitian immigrants start their lives in the United States this way.

Other obstacles face legal immigrants in their efforts to secure permanent jobs. Their chances of securing white-collar jobs are improved if they have a diploma from an American institution of higher learning. The same is true if they come from a city rather than a rural area: they are more familiar with city ways and are likely to be more aggressive in finding out what jobs are available. They are again in a better position if they have marketable skills, especially if they know English. As Alejandro Portes and Robert Bach (1980:317) write: "Knowledge of English is not a variable conventionally employed in human capital models of income, but it is a skill which seems particularly important for newly-arrived immigrants." I have found that with the exception of medical professionals, most Haitian-Americans, regardless of their class status in Haiti, begin here with lower-class status because they speak no English; when they know enough English, many are able to move upward. Of some importance in understanding the reasons that a Haitian-American worker is engaged in one type of job rather than another is the length of time the person has been in New York. The longer one has been here, the better one's chances of holding a good job, for one has had more time to acquire fluency in English and an understanding of the American job market.

The ethnic network is fully exploited in the search for a job. Usually a relative or friend helps the recent immigrant to locate a job, goes along to help during the job interview, and serves as a reference.

Relatives or friends tell the job seeker how to go about finding a job, explaining the possibilities open to recent immigrants. A relative or friend may ask his or her boss to give a job to the newcomer, especially if there is an opening and if the worker is well liked in the workplace. A worker who is leaving a job may pass it on to a friend.

In factories and in the home health-care field, many immigrant workers find their jobs through chain employment. It is common in the Haitian-American community for workers actively to seek jobs for unemployed friends and family members in the factories, stores, and homes where they work. In this fashion they build a support mechanism with the introduction of co-ethnics to the workplace. This procedure lessens the pressure on the newcomers, who then find someone nearby to help with English translation or to ride with to work. The Haitian experience seems to corroborate an earlier finding: "new immigrants of the same nationalities came in clusters, because whenever a job opened up in a shop, through their kin networks 'one pulled in another'" (Preston 1979:21). The workplace may be considered one more domain where Haitian-American ethnicity becomes manifest through an expression of solidarity among co-workers.

Some Haitian immigrants who know enough English go from one factory to another to apply for jobs, and some are successful.

Women who seek work as domestics—this sort of work is a refuge for illegal immigrants—get jobs through friends who already work for white families. The more relaxed ones place ads in the Sunday edition of the *New York Times*. When a prospective employer calls, they have someone translate the conversation for them and write down the caller's name and address.

The two Haitian neighborhood service centers, on Manhattan's West Side and in Brooklyn, provide legal aid to those who seek to change their immigration status, offer English classes and training on sewing machines, and serve as translation centers and placement offices. The staffs of these centers work hard to place job seekers with institutions or families that might give them affidavits of support so they may change their immigration status.

The Haitian-American churches also do their share to secure jobs for immigrants. The ministers and priests send job seekers to members of their congregations who are aware of openings, and among the parishioners prospective job seekers find the network of friends who may later help them find jobs. Church members are alert for available jobs and advise fellow churchgoers on how to apply for them. There is a considerable flow of communication about jobs within the network of church affiliation and secular voluntary associations.

The Workplace

Haitian immigrants use car pools, public transportation, and private cars to get to work. When several Haitians from the same neighborhood work in the same factory, a worker who has a car picks up the others who pay weekly fees to the driver. If all of them have cars, they alternate by the day or week. Someone who has a van may carry passengers to work every morning. This arrangement is found most often among people who commute to work in New Jersey. On the way to work they talk about their problems in New York, about the remittances they are sending to relatives in Haiti, and, if they trust each other, about Haitian politics.

In the workplace Haitians provide Creole translations for those who still have problems with English. Without this help, some of them would not be able to keep their jobs. They socialize with each other at work more than they did some years ago. In the 1960s they took care not to get too friendly with each other and avoided talk about politics for fear of reprisals against their families: any Haitian one did not know very well might be a government spy.[1] As Bill Thompson (1972:87) pointed out, "Among the Haitian community in New York, it is an article of faith that the [François] Duvalier machine has paid spies circulating among them. Anti-Duvalier talk, if reported to the ears of the dictator, can mean imprisonment or death for relatives still in Haiti." Haitian immigrants are more relaxed now and do not hesitate to joke about Baby Doc.

Before going to work most Haitian immigrants like to eat a solid meal, a simple continuation of a Haitian tradition. They believe that a morning meal of boiled green banana and eggs or meat keeps them in good health for the rest of the day. Some lower-class women take cooked food to work and share it with their compatriots after heating it on hot plates or in portable steamers or ovens. They seldom eat in cafeterias or fast-food establishments because of the expense, and in any case most of them do not care for American food.

By and large, Haitian workers get along well with their co-workers and are active members of labor unions. In 1978 a substantial number of Haitian workers held membership in the National Union of Hospital and Health Care Employees; the Hotel, Restaurant, and Club Employees Union; the Bedding, Curtain, and Drapery Workers Union; the Fur and Leather Machine Workers Union; the International Ladies Garment Workers Union; and the Amalgamated Clothing and Textile Workers Union. Very few of these workers had participated in unions in Haiti. Not all Haitian workers, however, are union members. Some have never joined a union; others have withdrawn their membership because they believe the unions are ineffective. As one informant put it, "I was a union member, but not any more. I lost interest because the

1. In his study of the Haitian community in Evanston, Ill., Teklemarian Woldemikael (1980:302) wrote: "They do not trust one another in political matters, and the expression of political views is reserved for their intimates. . . . They believe that the government has spies all over, and that they are spied upon even in Evanston."

union can't do anything for you. If it was well organized, it could help the worker. But now it is the same as the boss, two faces of the same coin" (Preston 1979:26).

The same report tells us that "the immigrants described two broad styles of control exercised by foremen, managers and owners: a protective paternalism on one hand, and workplace tyranny on the other" (Preston 1979:21). The relationship of undocumented Haitian workers with their supervisors can often be characterized as one of "manufacturing consent." Undocumented workers, afraid of being identified as such, "grow docile, anxious to please, willing to tolerate any exploitation to avoid deportation" (Preston 1979:3). Those silent workers often become the prey of unscrupulous managers who force them to work in dead-end jobs in calamitous conditions for low pay and with no fringe benefits. Union membership sometimes prevents such abuses.

Haitian-American Economic Enclaves

A growing number of Haitian-Americans have their own businesses. The 1978 Haitian-American Business Directory lists the names and addresses of about 200 Haitian-American businesses in the New York metropolitan area. These businesses provide employment mainly for members of the proprietors' families and for undocumented immigrants. Located in the heart of the Haitian-American residential concentrations, they serve the black and West Indian community almost exclusively.

Most of the people involved in family enterprises have had some business experience in Haiti. Sometimes they retain the names of their businesses in Haiti: Choucoune, Haïti Chérie, La Belle Créole, Boulangerie Saint-Marc. The reputation they gained in Haiti helps them attract a clientele in the Haitian immigrant community.

Haitian-American family-run enterprises include restaurants, dry cleaners, barbershops, laundromats, grocery stores, jewelry shops, photo shops, bakeries, real estate offices, beauty parlors, travel agencies, pharmacies, bookstores, garages, record shops, private medical clinics, and others. Some of these offices and shops operate only after 5:00 P.M. on weekdays and all day Saturday: the owners have full-time jobs elsewhere and keep the businesses for additional income.

Several associates sometimes take turns running a business, usually because they have full-time jobs elsewhere. All of the barbershops I visited function through the rotation of associates. Barbers work after regular business hours and on their days off from their regular jobs. As most Haitian immigrants work on weekdays, only one barber stays in the shop during the daytime; after 5:00 P.M. and on Saturday, all the barbers are on duty. This system allows them to keep the shop open almost every day.

Most Haitian-American businesses rely heavily on a Haitian-American clientele. Ulf Hannerz (1974:54) has remarked that "as far as access to resources is concerned, ethnicity has here served to provide protected niches for entrepreneurs within the ethnic groups, in that nonmembers have been more or less disadvantaged in competing for the same customers." The Haitian-American businesses I observed in New York flourish to the extent that they attract Haitian-American and Afro-American customers. This observation seems to be in line with a recent study that concludes that "the presence and residential concentration of so many American blacks in the American cities where West Indians live has . . . influenced their business achievements. West Indians in New York, for instance, have had a ready made rather large constituency for their enterprises: the American, as well as the West Indian, black community" (Foner 1979:292).

Some Haitian immigrant workers are engaged in underground employment in addition to their regular jobs. "Underground employment" designates here a job outside the channels of the mainstream American economy. Such employment can be permanent or temporary. The individual who participates in underground employment can be self-employed or an employee of someone else. As neither the employer nor the worker reports the income earned, no taxes are paid on it. This sort of employment is particularly attractive to undocumented workers and is widespread among legal residents as well.

An extensive network of relatives and friends is used to secure such jobs. Both employers and employees benefit: employees receive some income on which they pay no taxes and employers pay less than the minimum legal wage and save the cost of social security and other benefits.

Many Haitian-American women who do not have resident status undertake child care as underground employment. So do some retired and other unemployed women. This work requires no extra expenses, as parents who bring children to the woman's apartment for care by the day or week provide the food, diapers, and toys they will need. This arrangement is very convenient for families who live in buildings where such services are offered. Taking children to a public day-care center places a burden on the mother, especially during the winter months, when she must dress them warmly and take them to the center, often before dawn, before going to work. The advantage of taking the children to another apartment in one's own building is obvious. Aside from the convenience, scheduling is more flexible and the service is more personalized and less costly. The arrangement also has some disadvantages, however. The apartment where the children are cared for has little space in which they can play and no special equipment. The degree of hygiene is dubious at best. One spoon may be used, without washing, to feed all the children. And the children have no opportunity to learn English when everyone speaks Creole.

Some Haitian-American barbers and hairdressers serve their clients at home. In this way they do not have to qualify and pay for a state license. This is a personalized way of doing business. A client pays less for the services and can enjoy conversations with other Haitian-American clients. Tailors, masons, and carpenters follow a similar practice, engaging in side jobs among the ethnic community. These are basically weekend and day-off jobs. Haitian-American immigrants who engage in such work show great ingenuity in augmenting their weekly incomes.

Neighbor to Neighbor

Haitian-Americans let their relatives and friends know when a vacancy occurs in their apartment building. After ten years or so, the building is likely to be almost completely occupied by Haitian-American tenants. Thus a network of friends and relatives is established within a single building.

Haitian-American immigrants who live in the same building collaborate in a multitude of ways. Some buildings have a communal spirit; a flow of communication and visits from one apartment to another fosters continual emotional and economic support. One may get an interest-free loan from a building mate or borrow a neighbor's kitchenware. When one tenant gives a party, another brings chairs to augment the host's. Food is borrowed and shared. One may borrow a pint of milk from one neighbor, lend a cup of sugar to another. When a woman goes away for a weekend, a neighboring family may invite her husband and children to eat with them. If one's parents live in the building, they just drop in; if food is served, they get their share.

Favors are exchanged among building mates. People with no access to a car may ask a neighbor for a ride from time to time. The neighbor may even offer weekly rides for grocery shopping. The shopper may be asked to buy something for a neighbor. If the building belongs to a Haitian-American, the landlord is not likely to harass tenants who do not pay their rent on time. By the same token, the landlord may take some time before making needed repairs on the building.

Some apartments in such buildings are turned into private dining clubs. A person who lives alone may pay a family in the building a weekly fee, say $10 a week, to eat dinner with them, rather than cook after a day at work or eat alone at a Haitian-American restaurant. Single people who eat in a neighboring household have the opportunity to enjoy the company of other people, and the family is likely to care for them when they are sick.

The use of the telephone is another area of collaboration. Some Haitian-American households do not own a telephone and have to depend on a neighbor's. One circulates the neighbor's phone number as one's own, and makes and receives calls at the neighbor's apartment. The situation may become embarrassing, and some private phones are locked to prevent neighbors from using them for long-distance calls.

A few buildings function as total institutions. Among one's fellow tenants one can find a tailor, a car-pool driver, a mason, a barber, a hairdresser, a folk healer, a dressmaker, an electrician, and more. One can even buy one's clothing ready-made from a *revendeuse* or *madan sara* (retailer) in the building. These women buy clothing in various sizes at the factories where they work, and whenever there is a good sale somewhere, they buy enough merchandise to sell to their neighbors.

Buying a Home

Almost every Haitian-American immigrant wishes to buy a home, as a matter of status and security.[2] The status factor is implied in the informants' statement "Sé vagabon ki loué kay" ("Respectable people don't rent"). Owning a home is also a way of acquiring additional income—one rents an apartment to a tenant and uses the rent to pay the monthly mortgage—and of bringing members of the extended family together. It is common to find buildings in which married sisters, brothers, and other relatives live in separate apartments. The reasons that a Haitian-American likes to buy a house seem to be the same as for most immigrant workers and have been summed up this way: "To save the amount which he would have to pay in rent as a lodger. To obtain a steady source of income from rents by taking lodgers; in this way, he is able to supplement his income and eventually when he decides to sell, he makes a further profit as a result of rising prices. To express his achieved status as an immigrant who has made good" (Dahya 1974:103).

There are two general trends in the community in regard to buying homes. People who were members of the upper class in Haiti and professionals who sometimes wish to entertain American guests buy family homes in Queens. They are part of the white-collar middle class. These professionals—physicians, university professors, nurses, real estate agents, entrepreneurs—are found in great numbers in Queens. Haitian-Americans who buy houses as an additional source of income prefer to do so in Brooklyn, where cheap apartment buildings and two-family houses are available.

Haitian-American workers have developed productive strategies for each of the steps necessary to find a house, to pay the monthly mortgage, and to rent apartments in it. The first step, of course, is to save enough money for the down payment. For at least a few years before buying a house the family uses all possible means of saving money. They watch their food-consumption habits, whenever possible taking food from home to the workplace rather than going to a restaurant for lunch. Long-distance calls are curtailed, and they try in other ways to keep the phone bill to a minimum.

2. The acquisition of a home gives today's immigrant a sense of security, as it did for European immigrants to industrial America; see Golab 1977:32.

They may lock their phone to keep visiting neighbors from placing toll calls on it, though they will let them use it for urgent and serious matters. They may cut in half the amount of money they send to Haiti, and a relative who writes for money may be put off for a few months. Such a delay may discourage all the relatives from asking for money too often.

The second step is to find a good house to buy. For this task the buyers may rely on Haitian-American friends who know of a house for sale. If they have an acquaintance who is a real estate agent, they may do business with him. They ask for advice from friends and relatives who have had some experience with real estate. They may invite a Haitian-American mason to check the house's construction and may at this stage check with another Haitian-American real estate agent to find out if the price is fair. They will not make the decision until they have consulted with a number of people.

When they have decided on the house they want to buy, they may borrow money from relatives and friends or participate in one or more rotating credit associations. If they cannot get enough money in this way, they may apply for a bank loan.

Once they have the house, they look for tenants. Relatives and people who have lent them money are invited to move in first, if they want to do so. If not, they advertise their apartments through friends, relatives, and the church. They are selective in their choice of tenants, looking for *bon moun*, quiet people who will not complain if the apartments are sometimes cold in the winter.

The fifth and last step is to try to make the monthly mortgage payment without taking the money from one's own salary. The tenants' rent is supposed to cover the mortgage and the maintenance bills.

Despite the advice they seek from friends, most Haitian-Americans remain unfamiliar with the necessary differences between tropical and New York construction. Working people cannot afford to pay high prices, either, and good houses are not sold cheaply. In general, they do not make very good deals. What they buy is likely to bring them constant maintenance problems. Their houses are often in deteriorating areas and very old. One Haitian-American informant commented, "Buying a house in Brooklyn always ends up a bad deal emotionally and financially."

Rotating Credit Associations

Haitians who are accustomed to using rotating credit associations as a way of saving money (Laguerre 1978b, 1982a) continue to do so in New York City. Such associations are called in Creole *sangue, min,* or *assosié*. They are not peculiar to the Haitian-American experience. Similar rotating credit associations are found in Trinidad (Herskovits and Herskovits 1947), in the Bahamas (Crowley 1953), in Guiana (R. T. Smith 1953), in Jamaica (Katzin 1959), and in the Dominican Republic (Norvell and Wehrly 1969). They are believed to be a New World adaptation of a West African rotating credit association known as *esusu* (Bascom 1952).

Haitian-Americans are not the only Caribbean immigrants to have carried this institution with them from their homeland. Among Jamaicans in London "methods of saving vary, but the most prevalent is the friendly cooperative effort normally referred to by Jamaicans as 'partner'. . . . Fifteen or twenty people pay a weekly sum of between one pound and five pounds to the organizers. . . . The total amount at the end of each week goes to one of the twenty" (Hyndman 1960:74). There is also some indication that Bahamian immigrants in the United States have participated in rotating credit associations within their own ethnic enclaves. Indeed, "Bahamians returning from contract labor in the United States have reported that there are many *esu* operating in Florida, especially in the Bahamian communities in and near Miami. . . . They also report that *esu* have existed among contract laborers, mostly Bahamians and Jamaicans, while working even in the northern and western states" (Crowley 1953:80). The works of Ivan Light (1972) and Aubrey Bonnett (1980) give a good idea of the widespread use of these credit associations. In a study of their use by West Indian immigrants in Brooklyn, Bonnett (1980:277) found that "the first generation uses the money for basic urban necessities, such as buying furniture, clothing and other consumer goods. . . . Among the second generation there is a tendency to invest either in small business or in the purchase of one's home."

The Haitian-American *sangue* is an association in which "a lump sum fund composed of fixed contributions from each member of the association is distributed, at fixed intervals and as a whole, to each member of the association in turn" (Geertz 1962:243; see also Ardener 1964). The simplest form of *sangue* has about five members and no president (see Fig. 1*a*). Someone decides to form a *sangue* and invites friends and neighbors to join. They agree on the direction of the rotation. Each member in turn receives the contributions of the others. All members of the small acephalous *sangue* are likely to be Haitian-American. They know each other, and each knows where the others live. An atmosphere of trust among the participating members minimizes the chance of default. The first to receive the fund will be the first to receive it in the following rotation. The members may keep running the *sangue* without making any change in the direction of the rotation.

Some *sangues* elect a president to take charge of the transactions. The president and the members decide the way in which the fund should be rotated. In this form of *sangue*, the members may not know each other. Every week they take their contributions to the president, who passes the money on to the member whose turn it is to receive it (see Fig. 1*b*).

A single membership may be shared by two people. Each person pays half of the weekly contribution, and they share the fund equally when it is their turn to collect.

Some people hold two memberships in the same *sangue* or a single membership in each of two *sangues*. One may be the president of one *sangue* and simply a member of another, president of both, or a member of both. In any case, such people receive shares from two *sangues* or two shares from one.

In New York it is customary, though not obligatory, for the member who receives the fund to give a small amount to the president for the services he or she provides. It is not customary for the president to withhold a small amount from each member's contribution to cover the risk of a default, as seems to be the case in Guiana (R. T. Smith 1953:32) and the Dominican Republic (Norvell and Wehrly 1969:46). When someone defaults in New York, the entire membership suffers the consequences; the president is not held responsible. Informants complain that the risk of default is greater in *sangues* with mixed Haitian and Puerto Rican membership. The best way to avoid losing one's money, they be-

a. Acephalous *sangue*

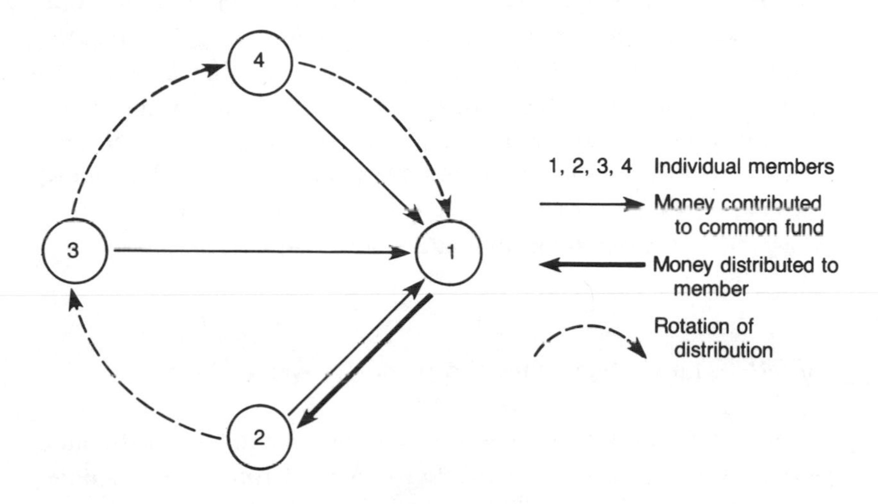

b. *Sangue* with president

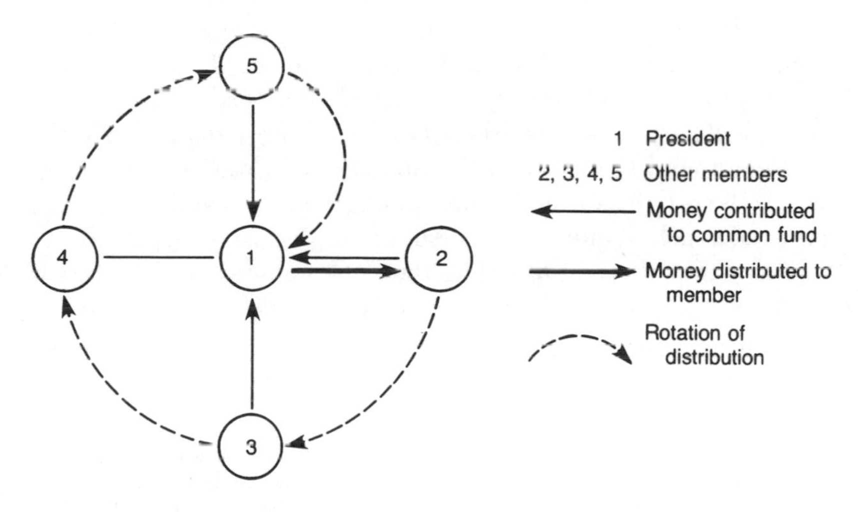

Figure 1. Forms of Haitian-American *sangue*

lieve, is to join a *sangue* only with members of one's own ethnic group.[3]

Sangues are most popular among undocumented Haitian immigrants, who are wary of opening checking and savings accounts because of the need to obtain a social security number and thus to reveal their identity to the government. This folk institution is also used by other Haitian immigrants, however, "to finance small businesses, to buy houses, to operate grocery stores, tailor shops, jewelry stores and real estate operations" (Bonnett 1980:271). Above all it is a way of accumulating some capital.

Borlette: The Haitian-American Numbers Game

Some Haitian-Americans—the number cannot be estimated—play numbers games in the hope of increasing their income. One variety, the *borlette*, is very popular in Haiti and is by far the most popular lottery in the Haitian-American community.[4] The games are owned and operated by Haitian-American immigrants.

The *borlette* operator, referred to as *bouqui* after a legendary figure in Haitian mythology, sells tickets numbered from 00 to 99. Three prizes are offered in each game. There are *ti bank* (small bank) and *gro bank* (big bank) *borlettes*. The *ti bank borlette*'s maximum fund is $100, and the operator sells each number only once. The *gro bank*'s fund is unlimited, the prices of the numbers vary, and each number may be sold to more than one person. As in Haiti, the operation of selling the same number to various people is called *pousé boul* (to push balls). The three winning numbers are determined by the last two digits of the winning numbers of the Dominican Republic's lottery, played every Sunday. Some

3. Monserratian immigrants in Britain have come to the same conclusion. "First, a member . . . who fails to keep up his or her payments is traceable. Unless he severs all ties with all Monserratians he will probably be readily found by other members. . . . A second major implicit sanction lies in the fact that the news of such a misdemeanour would be quickly communicated among Monserratians in London and also back to the home island" (Philpott 1968:471). I think that the same is true in the case of Haitian immigrants in New York.

4. The organization and functioning of *borlette* in Haiti is detailed in Laguerre 1982a.

immigrants participate also in a *borlette* that draws its winning numbers from the last two digits of the winning numbers of the semiweekly Haitian national lottery.

The operator decides how much money each number should be sold for and sets the amount of each prize. He negotiates with runners (people employed to sell numbers to prospective players) the amount they will receive for each game and decides whether or not the *pousé boul* will be allowed for a specific game. Before each game the runners deliver to him the money they have collected from the players.

The operator of a small *borlette* may be his own sole runner. He may place some money in a bank so that he can pay his clients if he is unable to sell all of his tickets on time; his reliability is crucial for his success. In general, the operator gets his clientele through his runners and friends. Owners of restaurants, stores, bookshops, and barbershops may be part of his network; their clients are likely to be invited to buy numbers. Selling numbers is one way to attract clients to one's store. Sometimes the *borlette* operator pays part of the rent on these places. Here we find similarities between the functioning of the *borlette* and that of the numbers game in the Afro-American community. "In order to keep up a semblance of respect for the law, about half the stations [in Chicago's black community] are fronted by legitimate businesses" (Drake and Cayton 1970:470). Often the clientele does not know for whom the runner works. Thus the racket remains a secret operation.

The winning numbers are announced through the various Caribbean newspapers that have large circulations in New York. A $1 *ti-bank borlette* ticket may win $10, $15, or $50. If all the numbers are sold, the owner takes in $100, distributes $75 in prizes, and shares the remaining $25 with his runners.

A few Haitian-American immigrants also play *bolita*, a Spanish-Caribbean numbers game. The *bolita* numbers go from 00 to 99, as in *borlette*, but only one prize is awarded. The holder of a winning $1 *bolita* ticket collects $60; the owner shares $40 with his runners.

Some Haitian-Americans also play a *borlette* game based on the American numbers game. Francis Ianni (1974:78) describes how the American game functions:

> All the customer has to do is pick a number from 1 to 999. Then he gives his number plus his money to a runner, the lowest man in the numbers hierarchy. . . . The runner hands the money over to a controller. . . . The controller disciplines the runners, keeps the accounts tabulated and passes the money up to the big man, the banker. . . . And then there is a fourth party that has to be cut in, the organization. . . . Only the organization has the money and the muscle to keep the cops and politicians from breaking up the game and shaking down the players and the operators.

The American numbers game consists of a three-digit number that is determined by a combination of winning horses at a specific racetrack. Some Haitian immigrants, however, play it like two-digit *borlette*, splitting a three-digit number into two two-digit numbers. One may split 367, for instance, into 36 and 67. The operator of the *borlette* must inform his clientele whether the winning numbers will consist of the first two or last two digits of the American number.

Borlette numbers are often selected on the basis of dreams. A Haitian book called *Chala* tells the numbers that correspond with objects seen in dreams. In that respect *borlette* players are no different from American numbers players.[5] "Since the nineteenth century, policy players have consulted 'dream books' to determine the numbers they should play for the day. These numerological tomes which are sold in small shops in the black community and in *botánicas* in Spanish speaking areas list a number for every symbol that may appear in a dream" (Ianni 1974:113). There are so many underground lotteries in New York, however, that once players have identified their numbers they sometimes have a hard time deciding which day to play them.

Players may also choose their numbers through simple calculations. One digit is added to or subtracted from each digit of the previous winning number. The number 75, for example, yields the following combinations:

+1	8	6
	7	5
−1	6	4

5. Good descriptions and analyses of the American numbers game may be found in Zola 1963:353–61, Carlson 1939, and Mayfield 1956.

Reading up and down as well as across, the player will choose either 86, 75, 64, 87, 76, 65, or 54.

Still other players use voodoo in their search for possible winning numbers. The voodoo priest may help them in matters related to voodoo symbolism. The voodoo factor facilitates the success of *borlette* games by giving the numbers played a supernatural significance and thus bolstering players' confidence. The use of voodoo by Afro-American numbers players has also been documented (McCall 1963). Numbers seen in movies or on cars involved in accidents are also used.

Whatever a number's origin, players usually also play its reverse and its *compaiel* (the following number in a sequence). The reverse of 15, for example, is 51. *Chala* gives two or three numbers for each dream item. If *Chala* gives 45 and 10 for dog, the player must take 45; its reverse, 54; and its *compaiel*, 10. Other combinations of numbers are also possible. One may add all the winning numbers of the week, for example, and divide the sum by 3. The position of the moon is also important in the selection of numbers. If *Chala* gives 12, 58, and 96 for black cat and if the moon is full, one plays 96: during a full moon one has to take the highest number in the sequence.

Playing the numbers obviously entails an economic risk. Because it is an underground activity, there is no possibility of redress in court if the owner fails to pay the money won. The community, however, has its own regulatory mechanisms. A *borlette* operator who fails to pay is likely to be pressured by his friends to do so. If he still fails to pay, gossip will usually end his career in the numbers business.

Those who benefit most from the numbers game are the operators and the runners. The chances of winning any game are always slim, and most players lose more than they win.

Ethnicity and Economic Adaptation

Most legal Haitian immigrants have come to this country to earn money, and they can be found in almost every sector of the U.S. labor force. Like the majority of immigrants everywhere, however, most Haitian immigrants seem to be concentrated in low-paying jobs with unpleasant working conditions (see Piore 1979:17).

No official statistics on the income distribution of Haitian immigrants are available. After interviewing sixty Haitian families in New York, I estimate that in 1978 the median income of legal workers was about $10,000 a year and of undocumented workers about $8,500 a year. In a nonrandom sample of fifty-four Haitian immigrants in New York, Patricia Elwell and her associates (1977:8) found that the average weekly wage was around $150, or $7,500 a fifty-week year. These estimates seem to corroborate those of an earlier study (Palmer 1976), which found that the median annual family income of Caribbean immigrants in the United States in 1970 was just under $8,300.

By now it is obvious that ethnicity plays a major role in the way in which Haitian immigrants organize their economic lives. It is through the manipulation of their ethnicity that they find jobs, organize rotating credit associations, operate businesses, and attract players to their numbers games. They play ethnic roles whenever such behaviors can be beneficial to their own interests. As Herbert Gans (1979:8) puts it, "ethnics have some choice about when and how to play ethnic roles."

Ethnic awareness is played out in the adaptive strategies that Haitian-Americans develop to secure employment. Sometimes they identify with Afro-Americans; at other times it is wiser to put forth their Haitian origin. Personal ethnic identity almost certainly comes into play during economic transactions and social interactions. Haitian-American job seekers, for example, may try to convince an Anglo-American employer that their minority status and their fluency in more than one language will be beneficial to the employer. A different strategy may be followed with a Haitian-American employer. Here job applicants are likely to stress the importance of ethnic solidarity for the well-being of the community, their personal interest in the employer's success, and the lack of communication problems between them.

Ethnicity is also used as a strategic factor in other economic endeavors. Organizers turn to co-ethnics to develop rotating credit associations in order to minimize the chance of default. *Borlette* operators recruit players among their compatriots, assuming that they are less likely than others to denounce them to the police.

The players, too, find it more convenient to deal with co-ethnics than with others.

Ethnicity is clearly a factor in the establishment and success of businesses in the Haitian-American community. As Ivan Light (1972:12) points out, "the special demands of ethnic consumers . . . [create] protected markets for ethnic tradesmen who [know] about the things their countrymen [want]." Haitian-American entrepreneurs are well aware of the consumer behaviors of their co-ethnics. They maintain their clientele by selling the kinds of goods and products that Haitian-Americans need and desire.

Ethnicity is one variable among others that helps to explain the economic adaptation of Haitian-American immigrants in New York City. It is manipulated in a number of ways by landlords and tenants, entrepreneurs and clients, employers and employees. It provides them with an identity that they use productively in transactions of varied importance.

[6]

Health Beliefs and Practices

The differences between the immigrants' health practices and the medical culture of mainstream American society point up their ethnic identity to observers and to themselves. Their subordinate status is also brought home to them by the frequent necessity to modify their ethnic behavior to conform with the mainstream American health-care system.

Unable to participate fully in the political economy of the United States, oppressed racial minority groups in urban America have developed various medical subcultures (M. Clark 1959, Garrison 1977, Snow 1977). Haitian-Americans continue to use home remedies in addition to the facilities of modern hospitals and the services of physicians of their own language and culture. The possibility of using both traditional and mainstream medicine has certainly helped the immigrants in their adaptation to urban America.

It is estimated that roughly 70 percent of the Haitian population in New York belong to the lower class. Obviously, some of the medical beliefs and practices described below are also relevant for middle- and upper-class Haitian immigrants. The health-care behavior of Haitian-Americans varies widely, however, as a result of differences in their past medical experience, their previous class status in Haiti, and their immigrant status in the United States.

Epidemiological Characteristics

No epidemiological study of the Haitian population in the United States has ever been carried out, partly because of the group's recent arrival and partly because of the illegal status of many of the immigrants. The Haitian Medical Association, with headquarters in New York and branches in various American and Canadian cities, has focused primarily on helping newly arrived Haitian physicians to secure jobs. Thus, apart from several brief reports on health practices among Haitian-Americans, no in-depth medical research has been published on the state of health of the Haitian immigrant population, and most statistical studies merge Haitians with other American blacks. Research carried out in Haiti on diet and nutrition, pellagra, tropical sprue, intestinal bacteria, and coronary and aortic atherosclerosis is of some relevance to our present concern, however.[1]

Selected Disease Patterns in Haiti

DIETARY DEFICIENCIES Since the 1950s a high incidence of anemia and multiple nutritional deficiencies has been observed among the rural population of Haiti in particular (see, for example, Sebrell et al. 1959). A nationwide study of 1,322 lower-class preschool children found that "the edema (or kwashiorkor) index was 7 percent, suggesting that, in this age group at this socioeconomic level and in the country as a whole, approximately one out of 14 children were likely to have been suffering from kwashiorkor in the summer of 1958 at the time of the survey" (Jelliffe and Jelliffe 1960:1365). Although these findings are now more than twenty years old, the protein and calorie deficiencies that cause kwashiorkor still exist in Haiti, and one can assume that a certain propor-

1. See, for example, Scott 1974, 1975, 1978; Weidman 1976, 1978; Bowering, Lowenberg, and Morrison 1980; Dambreville 1949; Comhaire and Comhaire 1952; Boulos 1954, 1955; Sebrell et al. 1959; Jelliffe and Jelliffe 1960, 1961; King 1964, 1967, 1975; King et al. 1963a, 1963b, 1966a, 1966b, 1968a, 1968b; Béghin et al. 1965a, 1965b, 1970; Dominique 1965; Sirinit et al. 1965; King and Price 1966a, 1966b; Duvalier 1968:451–67; Rawson and Berggren 1973; Ade 1978; Clark 1921; Klipstein and Samloff 1966; Klipstein et al. 1966; Groom 1961; Groom et al. 1959, 1964. Noël 1975: 157–72 reviews the literature on public health in Haiti.

tion of Haitian children brought to the United States suffer from this syndrome until they are able to compensate for their earlier deficiencies. A cultural factor that contributes to protein deficiency in children (and in women as well) is the unequal distribution of protein foods among family members. When meat is served, the major part goes to the husband on the assumption that he must be well fed to provide for the household. As Kendall King and his associates found in a nutritional survey of rural Haiti (1968b:118), "the problem is not one of net protein deficiency in the community, but rather unwise distribution of the protein among the members of the family." The same pattern of distribution persists among Haitian migrants in the United States.

In a study of family food consumption patterns among Brazilian sisal workers, Daniel Gross and Barbara Underwood found that "a disproportionate amount of available calories went to the wage earner in order to sustain his performance on the job. . . . It appears that the male subject ate approximately five-sevenths by weight of all the food available in the household. . . . Some sisal workers in Northeastern Brazil appear to be forced systematically to deprive their dependents of an adequate diet. The evidence shows that if they did not they could not function as wage earners" (1971:726, 731, 736). The same explanation seems to hold true in the case of Haitian workers. Today there is a common belief among Haitians that the man, whether he works or not, should be served the best portion of the meal, not only to help him maintain his physical strength, but also as a way of keeping him in the household, as he is presumed to be totally dependent on his wife for cooked food. The wife is presumed to be able to find alternative means of compensating for her own caloric deficiencies.

Recent studies on keratomalacia and xerophthalmia carried out in Haiti have found that vitamin A deficiency is one of the leading causes of binocular blindness among Haitian children (Sears 1972, Sommer et al. 1976). Although migrants to the United States do not typically come from the very poorest sectors of the Haitian population, special attention by clinicians to possible visual problems among members of this ethnic group seem warranted, particularly in view of the high number of self-reports of chronic "serious eye trouble" among Haitians in Miami, discussed below.

Any discussion of dietary deficiencies among Haitians must also take into account the presence of various endemic diseases on the island that significantly contribute to nutritional deficits over and above dietary factors. Tropical sprue, which is associated with vitamin B-12 and sometimes folate deficiencies, "is endemic in Haiti and plays a significant role in the development of the anemia and nutritional deficiencies which are frequently encountered" (Klipstein et al. 1966b:575). Parasitosis is also importantly implicated in nutritional deficiencies on the island. Both of these conditions may be encountered among Haitian immigrants and should be considered in the differential diagnosis of anemic patients (Meyers et al. 1977).

DISEASES OF THE CIRCULATORY SYSTEM On the basis of a comparison of a sizable postmortem population of American blacks from South Carolina and Haitians from around Port-au-Prince, Dale Groom and his associates conclude (1959:264): "First . . . the Negro in Haiti has about half the degree of coronary sclerosis that the American Negro has. Second, this proportion holds for both males and females and, roughly, for all age decades over 20. And third, no such disparity exists between the two populations as to the amount of aortic atherosclerosis." These researchers attribute the difference in the prevalence of coronary sclerosis in the two populations to differences in diet and life-style. "The Haitian consumes less of all foods of animal origin, and considerably less protein and fat [than the American black], with about three times as much of his total intake being in the form of linoleic acid" (p. 284). This claim is contradicted, however, by a dietary survey conducted in 1954, which observed a marked preference for animal fat among Haitian families (Boulos 1954). If consumption patterns of animal fats among American black and Haitian populations are indeed similar, differences in life-style between the two groups may nevertheless affect the metabolism of these foods. Thus Groom and his colleagues (1959) note that Haitians both sleep and exercise more than American blacks, and point to these habits as contributing to lower rates of coronary sclerosis.

The applicability of these findings to Haitian immigrants is difficult to assess. The physicians I interviewed were under the impression that they saw a considerable number of Haitian patients with heart and circulatory problems. As reliable statistics are unavailable, whether circulatory diseases have increased among Haitians in this country and whether any presumed increase may be due to postmigrational changes in diet are both moot points. It is my impression, however, that most Haitians have retained their island patterns of physical exercise, as most of them walk long distances to visit friends, to go to work, and to attend church services. Indeed, the island pattern has been reinforced in the United States, because many Haitians perceive public transportation in American cities to be unsafe. Thus, if circulatory diseases have increased among Haitians in this country, it is unlikely that changes in activity patterns are the principal cause. Dietary change, particularly among the younger generation of migrants, may be contributory, as junk foods have become common in this segment of the Haitian-American population.

Morbidity among Haitian-Americans

Because of the dearth of hard data on the mortality and morbidity rates of Haitians in the United States, we must rely for this information on the self-reports of acute and chronic conditions among a sample of Miami Haitians (Weidman 1978:325–449) and on the impressions of the Haitian physicians interviewed in New York.

In the Miami study the five chronic conditions that were most commonly reported by Haitian respondents on behalf of all members of their households during the preceding year were (in rank order) serious eye trouble, chronic skin trouble, nervous trouble and allergy (tied), and arthritis or rheumatism (Weidman 1978: 361). The most commonly reported acute conditions experienced in the preceding year were, as nationwide figures would lead one to expect, colds, influenza, and viral infections. In addition to these conditions incorporated in standard health-status lists, Hazel Weidman developed "ethnic symptom-condition lists" that probed the prevalence of culturally defined syndromes peculiar to each ethnic group. Within this list, the most frequently cited problems were "gaz or 'gas,' with 31 percent of the persons surveyed reporting it. Faiblesse (weakness/anemia) and vers (worms) were tied for second and third place. There was an equal response rate for coeur brulé (heartburn), mauvais sang ('restless,' 'moving,' or 'rising' blood), hyperacidité (hyperacidity), and colique (stomach cramps/abdominal pain), tying them in fourth to seventh rank at 8.6 percent" (Weidman 1978:436).

Many of the standard conditions reported, as well as the ethnic-specific symptoms, can be fully understood only in the context of certain Haitian cultural beliefs, which will be discussed in some detail below. Nevertheless, it is important to recognize that these self-reports show a correspondence with some of the diseases reported above as being common in Haiti itself (the self-reports of chronic eye and skin trouble, for example, in view of the aforementioned epidemiological studies of nutritional deficiencies, and "worms" in view of parasitosis).

Haitian physicians in New York present a somewhat different picture of morbidity among Haitian-Americans. The problems with this information are, of course, manifold. In addition to the fact that separate files and thus specific figures are not kept for Haitian patients, each physician's sample of cases tends to be biased by his own medical specialty, by the socioeconomic status of his clientele, and by the obvious omission of untreated cases from the sample. For what it is worth, however, the physicians report the following diseases as being most prevalent among their Haitian-American patients: diabetes, hypertension (severe and benign), stomach ulcers, and arthritis. Isolated cases of malaria are also found, and parasitosis is detected among children who have recently migrated from Haiti and among children who have eaten food that people have brought to the United States from Haiti.

The New York physicians report other diseases as posing particular problems because of the manner in which they are presented for treatment. Late presentation, for example, seems to be common for a number of conditions for various reasons. People suffering from hydrocele (*maklouklou*) usually delay seeing a physician out of a sense of shame about the condition; people who have cancer (especially of the cervix) tend to seek medical help only after the disease is beyond control, because Haitians tend not to consult physicians unless they experience pain. As a result, the prevalence of untreated cancer is assumed to be quite high in this ethnic group.

According to the physicians' reports, venereal diseases are also treated quite commonly among lower-class Haitian patients, as are bladder and prostate infections among men. People who suspect that they have a venereal infection, however, often secure an injection of penicillin from a friend who works in a hospital. As these suspected cases are treated without laboratory diagnosis and with no follow-up treatment, they are rarely cured. Various local infections, as well as the psychological stress of the immigrant experience, may also account for complaints of impotence among Haitian-American men.

The New York physicians interviewed were unanimous in reporting that the incidence of tuberculosis in the Haitian-American population is low. Moreover, as legal residents who may have had the disease in Haiti were necessarily cured in order to have been eligible for permanent residence in the United States, the reported cases all seem to have been contracted in New York. This assumed low rate of tuberculosis among Haitian-Americans may, however, be due to patients' culturally conditioned interpretations of the symptoms of this illness, which may well lead to a failure to seek health care. Thus rural Haitians have been reported to use the word *tuberculose* to cover a narrower range of symptoms than are covered by the word "tuberculosis."

> In the indigenous medical system this term [*tuberculose*] is associated only with those symptoms which modern western medicine labels "advanced active pulmonary tuberculosis." The other symptoms included in our general label "tuberculosis" are spanned by three other categories in Creole, none of which is considered serious. . . . The term "tuberculose" does not subsume those symptoms which western medicine identifies as "primary tuberculosis." Haitians do not believe "tuberculose" is found in children. [Wiese 1974:361]

It is likely that with this understanding of tuberculosis symptoms, Haitian patients seek help only when the disease is quite advanced.[2] Fear of the disease, which many poor rural Haitians have almost certainly observed to be fatal in a considerable number of cases, also inhibits them from seeking treatment.

2. Jean Wiese (1971) has provided an extensive analysis of Haitian ways of dealing with tuberculosis and an elaboration on the meaning of tuberculosis for rural Haitians. Two recent studies of tuberculosis among Haitian immigrants are Laven 1977 and Pitchenik et al. 1982.

Concepts of Disease and Illness

Concepts of Health

The activities that Haitians in Miami consider most important for maintaining health are eating well, giving attention to personal hygiene, and keeping regular hours. Prayer and good spiritual habits were reported by 8 percent of the Haitians sampled as being important to good health (Weidman 1978:311–12).

Haitians consider fat people to be both healthy and happy; thin people are believed to be in poor health, wasted by psychological and emotional problems. Thus Haitian dietary habits are closely related to ideas of physical and emotional well-being.

In addition to having "cold" and "hot" qualities, foods are considered to be either "light" or "heavy." The "heavy" types, such as corn meal, boiled plantains, and potatoes, should be eaten during the day and are said to provide the necessary caloric requirements for daily work. The "light" types of food, such as chocolate, bread, and soup, should be eaten for dinner. The method of preparation affects the classification of foods as well; boiled green bananas, for example, are "heavy," while fried yellow bananas are "light."

Because of their work schedules, Haitian-Americans are generally unable to continue all of their nutritional customs and practices in the United States. As they spend most weekdays away from home, they eat whatever is available near the workplace unless facilities are available for heating food brought from home. Contrary to their traditional dietary habits, many now eat their main meal at night, like most other Americans, and a "heavy" meal has consequently replaced the traditional "light" supper.

Haitians believe that not all foods are good for the human body at all times; the use of food must be in harmony with the individual life cycle. There are foods for babies, foods for adults, foods for menstruating women, foods for the sick, and foods for the elderly. Some foods can be eaten by people of all ages, but they vary in the manner of preparation or the quantity consumed. Some foods are forbidden to people at various stages of the life cycle; teenagers, for example, are advised to avoid much orange or lemon juice, so as not to develop acne. Pregnant women are particularly subject to food taboos and special food practices (César 1955,

Wiese 1976:196). They are encouraged to *manger pour deux* ("eat for two") and may therefore gain considerable weight during pregnancy. They are cautioned to avoid spices, but red fruits and vegetables (such as beets and pomegranates) are thought to build up the baby's blood.[3]

Degrees of Illness

Illness episodes range across a continuum from transitory disturbances to grave situations. A Haitian-American may thus characterize his or her illness in one of six ways:

1. *Kom pa bon* ("I do not feel well"). The illness does not confine the sufferer to bed. It is a transitory disturbance, and the individual should soon be well.
2. *Dé tan zan tan moin malad* ("I feel sick from time to time"). A complaint about the general state of health.
3. *Moin an konvalésans* ("I am convalescing"). The person has been sick but is now recuperating.
4. *Moin malad* ("I am sick"). The illness is not life-threatening.
5. *Moin malad anpil* ("I am very sick"). The person is in critical condition.
6. *Moin pap réfè* ("I will never be well again"). The patient expects to die.

Etiological Concepts

In one of the earliest papers on ethnomedicine in Haiti, Alfred Métraux observed (1953:28) that rural Haitians believe that illness can be of supernatural or natural origin. Natural illnesses are known as *maladi péi* (country diseases) or *maladi bon dié* (diseases of the Lord), and are believed to be of short duration. Supernatural illness appears suddenly, without any previous sign of discomfort. Thomas Dow (1965) has confirmed some of Métraux's observations.

3. Food taboos and their effects on the health of teenagers and pregnant, lactating, and menstruating women are discussed further in Béghin et al. 1970 and Marcelin 1954.

> The common cold, which occurs so frequently, is seen as a natural occurrence, but madness is seen as exceptional and often as supernatural in origin. . . . Supernatural illness is thought by the Haitian to be caused either by the loa (familial spirits) or by the Dead. . . . He must placate his ancestors by offering them a feast called a manger morts at certain intervals. If he does not, misfortune and illness are likely to befall him. [Dow 1965:40–41]

Spirits are thus the prime source of supernatural illnesses. Among illnesses of "natural" origin, six traditional conceptions of cause can be specified: (1) type (volume, quality, and color) and movement (directionality) of the blood; (2) location and movement of "gas" (*gaz*) in the human body; (3) type (quality) and movement (directionality) of milk in the female body; (4) hot/cold disequilibrium and movement of heat and cold in the body; (5) bone displacement; and (6) the movement of diseases. Though Haitians often perceive illness as caused by factors external to the body ("cold" or "hot" air and foods, "gas," spirits), a view that seems complementary to the germ theory of disease, few Haitians of lower socioeconomic status use the intrusion of germs as an explanation of illness.

Supernatural Causes of Illness: Spirits

Several types of illness are believed to be of supernatural origin, caused by angry spirits. Voodoo theology provides a theory to explain the occurrence of such illnesses (see Laguerre 1979b, 1980b). Each voodooist family has a spirit protector whose role is to protect its members from the malevolent power of other spirits. When one is initiated into voodoo, one must sign, so to speak, a pact with one's spirit protector. Spirits expect their protégés to offer a ceremony every year in their honor. The annual ceremony is a basic requirement for maintaining a good relationship with one's spirit protector. Individual spirits, however, may add other requirements in accordance with their own wishes and their positions in the spirit hierarchy. Without this kind of recognition, a spirit may be the object of other spirits' mockery, and may lose standing in the spirit hierarchy. To maintain good standing, spirits must show that they have followers, that they are able to protect those followers from other spirits and cure them when they are sick, and that the protégés recognize their power and are afraid of them. Spirits whose protégés demonstrate their respect and fear by offering a ceremonial meal in their honor every year have the respect and fear of other spirits as well.

There is thus a relationship of dependence between spirits and protégés. The protégés depend on the spirits for protection, especially for health, and the spirits depend on their protégés to maintain their status in the spirit hierarchy. The protégés, however, are always subordinate to the spirits.

Illness may occur whenever one gives other spirits an opportunity to make fun of one's spirit protector, as by failing to offer the annual meal. Illness thus becomes a punishment. A spirit may "send an illness" on a protégé or may neglect to intervene if another spirit decides to bother the protégé. Proper propitiation, however, may cause the spirit protector to relent.

Such an illness is diagnosed by a voodoo priest. The priest may be able to find out through spirit possession the reasons for the spirit's anger. During the possession trance, the spirit may explain why he or she is not happy with the protégé, the nature of the illness, and what the protégé must do to get well again. The spirit also informs the patient about the medication to be taken after the proper ritual duties have been performed.

While spirit protectors are likely to inflict physical illness on their protégés, the spirits of dead relatives take a more psychological approach to make their kin remember them. By appearing in dreams to remind relatives of their ritual duties (see Bourguignon 1954), they usually upset the dreamers sufficiently to cause them to provide a ceremony in honor of the dead.

Some illnesses are primarily the domain of voodoo healers. A type of hypertension can be cured, according to some people, only by voodoo priests. The spirit of a dead person sits on the neck of the patient (*mo chita dèyè noa kou moun nan*), and only a voodoo priest may rid the sufferer of the spirit. A handicapped patient who drools is believed to be the unwilling carrier of the spirit of a dead child; such a person is subject to voodoo treatment.

In short, illness of supernatural origin is fundamentally a breach in rapport between an individual and his or her spirit protector. It is a response from the spirit to that breach, a way of reprimanding the protégé. In such a situation, health can be recovered if the patient takes the first step of finding out the nature of the illness through the help of a voodoo priest and then follows the advice subsequently given by the spirit itself. Voodoo is thus both a religious and a medical system.[4]

Natural Causes of Illness

BLOOD IRREGULARITIES By far the most dangerous types of illnesses are believed to be caused by irregularities in the blood, and beliefs about the blood are extensive among Haitians. Indeed, Weidman has called blood "the central dynamic in Haitian understandings of bodily functioning and pathological processes" (1978: 522; see also 529–35). To a Haitian, blood can be *cho* (hot) or *frèt* (cold); *clè* (thin), *fèbl* (weak), or *épè* (thick); *sal* (dirty), *noa* (dark), or *jo-n* (yellow).

San cho (hot blood) provokes high fever, while *san frèt* (cold blood) is the result of malaria. Métraux discusses a similar classification of fevers (1953:53), although he does not discuss the symptomatology of each type. The blood is believed to regulate the hot/cold state of the body. The blood is said to be hot when a person becomes nervous or engages in heavy intellectual activity, and when one is sleeping or doing physical exercise. The body of a woman is hot during the weeks after childbirth. Blood is cold, however, when one is quiet and in a resting position, although resting itself is not a guarantee of cold blood. For if a person worries about personal problems while in a resting position, the upper part of the body will purportedly have warm blood and the lower part cold blood.

San clè (thin blood) causes pallor, and *san fèbl* (weak blood) physical or mental weakness (Dow 1965:42). When the blood is weak, one is advised to eat red foods (red meat, sugar beet) and drink red beverages, such as *siro pié bèf* (a syrup made of cows' legs and sugar). The blood becomes thick (*épè*) when one is frightened (*sézisman*) and remains this way when one is suffering from hypertension. Thick blood also causes *san piké* or *pikotman* (itching).

San jo-n (yellow blood) is caused by bile flowing in the blood,

4. Most of the scholarship on voodoo has focused on its religious aspect. There is now some interest, however, in voodoo as a medical system; see Delbeau 1969, Conway 1978, Scarpa 1975, Daniel 1977.

and *san noa* (dark blood) is a sign that the patient is about to die of an incurable disease. *San sal* (dirty blood) and *san gaté* (spoiled blood) are both associated with venereal disease and skin eruptions (Weidman 1978:377). *San gaté* has also been reported to result from fright (*saississement*: Métraux 1953:58) and thus seems similar to *mové san* (bad blood), which is attributed to fright and is associated with skin eruptions.

Blood is also believed to be capable of turning into water, particularly as a result of drinking too much alcohol. The occurrence of such a situation is believed likely to cause pleurisy or tuberculosis.

In addition to these various qualities of the blood itself, Haitians may attribute illness to irregularities in blood flow. Thus fear and fighting are both believed to cause blood to flow to the head, an occurrence that in turn is viewed as the cause of hypertension (Weidman 1978:320). *Pèdi san* refers to loss of blood through menstruation; menstrual irregularities (either profuse bleeding or irregular menstrual periods are referred to as *san kap boulvèsé*.

Gas (*Gaz*) Many Haitians believe that "gas" may provoke pain and anemia. Gas can occur in the head, where it enters through the ears; in the stomach, where it comes in through the mouth; and in the shoulder, back, legs, or appendix, where it may travel from the stomach. When gas is in the stomach, the patient is said to suffer a *kolik* (stomach pain), and gas in the head (*van nan tet*, also called *van nan zorey*—literally "gas in the ears") is believed to cause headaches. When gas moves from one part of the body to another (*gaz kap maché nan do-m*), pain is produced. Thus gas traveling from the stomach to the legs produces *doulè rimatis*, *frédi*, or *fréchè* (rheumatism); to the back, *do fè mal* (back pain); and to the shoulder, *gaz nan zépol* (shoulder pain). A tea made of garlic, cloves, and mint, or such solid foods as plantain and corn, are usually advised as treatment for these conditions, as they are believed to be capable of expelling gas.

To keep gas from entering the body, one must be careful about eating certain foods, such as leftovers (*mangé domi*), and especially leftover beans. After childbirth, women are particularly susceptible to the entry of gas, and must tie a belt or piece of linen tightly about the waist to keep it out. Gas is also believed to become warm, hot, or cold, but I was unable to get information on the associated health problems that such states may cause.

Movement of Milk The milk of a lactating mother is believed to be stored in her breast, and the mother must eat very well to be able to deliver healthy milk to her child. Although the milk nourishes both the mother and the baby, it can also be detrimental to the health of both if it is too thin or too thick. When the milk is too thick, it is said to cause impetigo (*bouton*). It can become too thin when a mother is frightened; fear causes the milk to move to her head, producing an acute headache or postpartum depression in the mother and diarrhea in the baby, if the child has been breast-feeding.

Hot/Cold Disequilibrium Illness is also believed to be caused when the body is exposed to an imbalance of cold (*frèt*) and hot (*cho*) factors. "Hot" and "cold" may or may not apply to temperature. Table 5 presents the Haitian categorization of foods in this system. Although not all of these foods are available in the United States, the diet of many Haitians in this country still includes them. Though there appears to be some consensus on the hot/cold qualities of most of the tropical fruits and staples used in the daily diet in Haiti (Wiese 1976:196), the views of immigrants in New York vary on the hot/cold states of the foods available in supermarkets.

Wiese found that life states are also classified as hot and cold in rural Haiti: "The scaling of a particular body state appears to be related to reproductive capacity. A female is always warmer than a male; a younger person always warmer than an older" (1976:198).

In this system of causation, illness is seen as being provoked by an imbalance of hot and cold factors. Thus cold and hot experienced in rapid succession may provoke *chofrèt* (cold or pneumonia). A woman who has just ironed her hair and then opens a refrigerator is likely to become a victim of *chofrèt*; so is a person who eats something "cold" after strenuous physical exercise. Eating "cool" tomatoes or white beans after childbirth is believed to induce hemorrhage, and "cold" orange juice is avoided in cases of menstrual disturbance. Often patients decide that they have *chofrèt* when they break out in a cold sweat during a fever.

Table 5. Haitian hot/cold classification of foods

(−3) Very Cold	*(−2) Quite cold*	*(−1) Cool*
Avocado	Banana	Cane syrup
Cashew nuts	Cashew	Custard apple
Marfrane cheese	Lime	Chayote fruit
Coconut meat	Grapefruit	Orange juice
Coconut juice mixed with milk	Lime juice	Tomato
Coconut juice	Okra	
Granadilla flesh	Orange	
Granadilla juice	Watermelon	
Mango		
Pineapple		
Soursop fruit		
Star apple		
Cassava bread		

(0) Neither hot nor cold: neutral		*(+1) Warm*
Banana juice	Goat meat	Eggs
Beef	Kidney beans	Grapefruit juice
Beets	Lima beans	Pigeon meat
Biscuits (of imported white flour)	Malanga	
Breadfruit	Cow's milk	
Cabbage	Goat's milk	
Mint candy	Parsley	
Carrot	Roasted peanuts	
Sweet cassava	Pigeon peas	*(+3) Very hot*
Foreign cheese	Plantain	
Chicken	Plantain gruel	Cinnamon
Coconut candy	Pork	Coffee (roasted)
Conch	Sweet potato	Nutmeg
Milled corn	Brown rice	"Clairin" (raw rum)
Marionade (fried dough balls)	White rice	Rum
Eggplant	Rice and mushrooms	
River fish	Non-iced soft drinks	
Sea fish	Imported Spam	
Grunion	White and yellow yams	
	Pumpkin	
	Sugar cane	

SOURCE: H. Jean C. Wiese, "Maternal Nutrition and Traditional Food Behavior in Haiti." Reproduced by permission of the Society for Applied Anthropology from *Human Organization* 35(2):193–200, 1976.

According to this system, a patent or herbal medicine of the class opposite to that of the disease is administered. Cough medicines, for example, are considered to be in the hot category, while laxatives are in the cold category. A person who has a cold is "hot" and needs to take a "cold" medicine. Someone with "cold" blood may have to take a "hot" medication to regulate body heat, and vice versa. Some migraines are believed to be due to an excess of heat and blood in the patient's head. To cure such an illness, one needs to take a "cold" medicine to lower the heat and bring the blood back to its normal position.

BONE DISPLACEMENT (*Zo déplasé*) Three types of "bone displacement" (*entorse*, sprain; *kou viré*, twisted or stiff neck; and *biskèt tonbé*, displaced vertebra) cause sufficient pain and discomfort to warrant health care. The proper practitioner to treat this kind of ailment is not a medical doctor, however, but a folk healer/chiropractor. These ailments are treated by physical manipulation of the affected part, sometimes accompanied by warm poultices and prayer.

MOVEMENT OF DISEASES Diseases, whatever their primary causes, may expand or move from one part of the body to another. When a disease has migrated from its primal position, it may cause pain in the area that it has reached. The notion of expansion and relocation of disease seems to be important in Haitian conceptions of illness, both as an explanatory device and as a motivation for seeking treatment.

Two Concepts of Illness

Weidman (1978) has reviewed a large number of Haitian terms for various symptoms and conditions and has concluded that the central Haitian folk concept of illness involves a disruption in the balanced state of the blood. Various kinds of internal and external disruptions to the system are labeled by special terms. Some of these terms (congestion, indisposition)[5] are similar to words used in standard biomedical terminology, and some are generally unknown to mainstream health professionals.

FRIGHT Fright, called *sézisman* in Creole (*saisissement* in French), is a disruption to the system caused by a sudden shock,

5. The occurrence, etiology, and treatment of "indisposition" are discussed in Philippe and Romain 1979 and Charles 1979.

such as the announcement of bad news or a sudden threat to one's physical well-being. Such a disruption may also be caused by indignation after one has been a victim of injustice (Métraux 1953: 58). When *sézisman* occurs, the blood is said to move to the head and may cause partial loss of vision or headaches. Lactating women are considered particularly susceptible to this illness, and it is believed to affect their milk in various ways. It is also believed to cause a temporary mental disturbance (*folie passagère*). Belief in *sézisman* and manifestations of it are common among Haitian-Americans in both Miami (Weidman 1978:517) and New York.

OPPRESSION The term "oppression" is used by Creole speakers to refer to asthma, although the exact referent differs somewhat from that of the biomedical term. According to Weidman, oppression "include[s] more than asthma. In many instances, oppression for Haitians seems to describe a state of anxiety and hyperventilation instead of asthma" (1978:448). Although the French term *asthme* is generally known to Creole speakers, and rendered as *sma* (Weidman 1978:448), it is not frequently used. Oppression is considered to be a cold state, as are many respiratory conditions.

Becoming Ill

Natural and supernatural illnesses have their own modalities and singular features that allow for their diagnosis. A "natural" illness is one with familiar symptoms and a determinate duration. Such illnesses, known as "diseases of the Lord" (Dow 1965, Métraux 1953), are not considered to be the result of any breach of contractual agreements with spirits. Illnesses of supernatural origin, however, are believed to appear suddenly, and once they appear, if nothing is done, they progress slowly through the body.

The way in which Haitians perceive and evaluate "natural" symptoms depends in part on their socioeconomic status, their past illness experience, and whether or not they had access to a physician when they were in Haiti. Employed people are less likely to seek medical attention than the unemployed, for fear of losing a day's pay;[6] thus it is likely that working people are more

6. A similar observation has been made concerning lower-class black Americans (Spector 1979:241).

tolerant of symptoms. Certain symptoms that are regarded with shame (hydrocele, epileptic seizures, the lesions of venereal disease) may also be tolerated longer before medical attention is sought. Many sick people hesitate to see a physician because they are more or less convinced that their illnesses are temporary. Through proper diet, vitamins, patent medicines, and home remedies, patients expect to cure themselves.

Experience with illnesses among one's close relatives seems to be of central importance in the evaluation of illness, whether one is of the lower or upper class: one's own symptoms are evaluated in light of the symptoms previously experienced by one's kin. The following case history exemplifies such an evaluation.

Joseph, a former teacher at a lycée in Port-au-Prince, migrated to New York in 1970. After his arrival he worked in a gas station. For some time Joseph had not been feeling well. His complaints included poor eyesight and physical weakness, which he attributed to hard work. What bothered him most was a small sore on his leg that did not heal. Joseph spent a lot of time reviewing his relatives' illnesses with them in order to discover if his own symptoms were similar to theirs. He particularly sought the counsel of his sister and aunt, as Haitian women are generally more knowledgeable about symptoms and cures than men. After consultation with members of his extended family, Joseph decided that his illness was not grave and that it was therefore unnecessary for him to see a physician. He had ruled out diabetes as a diagnosis, because neither his father nor his mother had had the disease. He was unsure, however, about the sickness that had terminated his father's life. Joseph's own diagnosis was "gas," and he was taking a home remedy for it. After falling into a coma, however, he was taken to the hospital and diagnosed as diabetic.

In such instances of self-diagnosis, the two symptoms to which Haitians most commonly attend are *douleur* (pain) and *faiblesse* (weakness). (Weidman 1978:495–96 includes dizziness and stiffness as well.) One Haitian physician reported that after years of practicing medicine among Haitian-Americans, he had concluded that Haitian-American medical care revolves around the treatment of "pain" and "weakness."

In clinical situations patients generally locate pain vaguely. Because of a belief among Haitians that when one is ill, the whole body suffers, the location of pain at a particular moment is not particularly important, especially since diseases may shift position. In addition, the causes of pain that are suggested by patients do not usually comport with biomedical ideas of causation ("gas," for example).

Physical weakness is taken as a sign of anemia or insufficient blood. A patient who fears anemia may complain to the physician, "I do not feel like eating" (Bouch moin an mè), or "I cannot work" (Pa kab travay). As these symptoms are usually attributed to a poor diet, patients may turn to vitamins in order to regain their strength. In general, symptoms tend to be interpreted by Haitians of low educational attainment in terms of folk medical concepts rather than biomedical concepts.

Coping with Illness outside the Mainstream Medical System

Uneducated and lower-class Haitian-Americans have five alternatives to choose from in their efforts to secure health services: (1) home remedies that they are aware of themselves or that are provided by family and friends, (2) modern medicine in either a hospital or a private clinic, (3) a nonvoodooist folk healer, (4) voodoo medicine, (5) a return trip to Haiti to see a family physician or voodoo healer there. Often a Haitian tries home remedies first, then sees a folk healer, and finally seeks help from a voodoo healer if one is available. Because of the expense, a physician may be sought only as a last resort. When a child is sick, however, parents do not usually wait long before consulting a physician; they may delay only if they suspect that the illness is due to teething.

Home Treatment

Most first-generation Haitian-Americans turn first to home remedies in treating illness. Lorimer Denis (1963) and Arsène Pierre-Noël (1959) have compiled lists of the most common remedies used by Haitians of lower educational and economic status. In New York City, however, some educated Haitians also used these remedies.

Such symptoms as fever, diarrhea, and constipation are usually treated with home remedies. Parents may also administer "worm medicine" to their children, either as a precautionary measure or as a cure. Weidman (1978:413) writes that "some Haitian mothers would diagnose 'worms' when children gave any indication of suddenly jerking during sleep, of sleep-walking, or when they cried during their sleep. In the last instance, the assumption was they cried because of 'belly pain.'" As we have seen, people may also describe their symptoms to family members and friends in order to learn about medications that have proved effective in treating a similar condition in the past. In such cases the illness may be diagnosed *de tête* (without physical examination) and the patient advised to take a prescription medicine that a relative or friend has used in Haiti or is taking currently. If necessary, a person may ask relatives back home to send medication for the condition; such medication can consist of leaves, roots, or French-manufactured products that have not been approved for sale in the United States. A good number of migrants believe in the efficacy of French medications (such as Kafénol for headache) that are in use in Haiti.

Within the household, the mother or grandmother and sometimes the father take responsibility for diagnosing symptoms. They keep alive the family's therapeutic tradition, some of it consisting of information that has been passed on from parents to children for generations. Today, however, conflicts sometimes arise between first- and second-generation family members when the latter want to see a physician but are required instead to take home remedies prepared by their elders. In New York older Haitians have lost their traditional expertise in advising on nutritional matters because they lack knowledge about American foodstuffs.

When everything advised by family and friends has been tried and the patient is still not cured, the same people will then recommend a visit to a physician, folk healer, or voodoo priest.[7]

7. The decision-making process of Haitian immigrants in matters related to health can be seen in Eliot Freidson's discussion of folk medical culture (1966:263): "The whole process of seeking help involves a network of potential consultants, from the intimate and informal confines of the nuclear family through successively more select, distant, and authoritative laymen, until the professional is reached. This network of consultants, which is part of the structure of the local lay community and which imposes form on the seeking of help, might be called the lay referral structure."

One's decision here is often influenced by one's immigration status, one's economic circumstances, and one's access to a voodoo priest. For to be sick means to be unable to work, and absence from work means the loss of a paycheck. For migrants who have no health insurance and whose illegal status prevents them from applying for Medicaid, the possibility of seeking help from a hospital or private physician is remote; thus a home remedy, a folk healer, or a voodoo priest is the preferred mode of treatment.[8] As a secondary resource, illegal immigrants consult a Haitian physician before going to a hospital.

Folk Healers

Although most "natural" illnesses are referred to either a folk healer or a medical doctor, some such illnesses—abscess, ulcer, *san gaté* (spoiled blood)—are thought to require the attention of both types of practitioner. Other illnesses belong exclusively to the domain of the folk healer. Although such healers may also be voodooists, these conditions require no voodoo rituals for a cure. *Entorse* (sprain) is one such condition; another is *lalouèt tonbé* (acute respiratory distress, attributed to the obstruction of the trachea by the uvula). Treatment by a folk healer is free; the patient must give the healer a small rock in lieu of payment.

Folk healers use three diagnostic techniques. They may first inquire about the history of the illness: the length of time the person has been sick, the location and characteristics of the pain, whether it is acute or periodic, what the patient has eaten. A folk healer may also examine the patient's eyes, hands, and skin color for indications of the state of the blood. The third technique, *man-yin* (touching), consists of palpating various parts of the body to ascertain whether a displaced bone or internal organ needs to be placed

8. Haitian-Americans are not the only ethnic group in America that continues to use both Western and folk medicine. Sicilian-Americans, for example, seek "the advice of both physicians and local curers, but the longer the illness [continues] and the greater the doubt about the diagnosis, the greater [becomes] the inclination for folk curing" (Grossman 1976:141; see also M. E. Smith 1972). The use of folk medicine among Afro-Americans, Chinese-Americans, Haitian-Americans, Italian-Americans, Mexican-Americans, Navajos, and mainland Puerto Ricans is discussed in Harwood, ed., 1981.

in its proper position. The medication or other therapy the healer prescribes is based on the diagnosis that results from the examination.

Folk healers usually recommend dietary supplements or restrictions. I have already discussed the use of plantains and certain teas to treat "gas," and the hot/cold system may also be the basis of the choice of foods recommended or restricted for therapeutic purposes. Folk healers commonly massage the patient with either burned alcohol or hot oil to treat a dislocation or sprain; sores and inflammations are treated with compresses, poultices, or baths. As in the home, laxatives are often prescribed, ostensibly to clean the intestinal tract and blood of impurities (particularly in cases of "dirty blood"). A laxative may be followed by an enema (*lavement*) to make sure no impurities remain. Dow describes an array of treatment procedures and curing techniques used by folk healers:

> In treating natural illness, the hungan uses such methods as baths, powders, and mixtures of herbs. Most hungans have an extensive knowledge of the native herbs and use them both externally and internally. . . . Massage is always directed toward the extremities. . . . These treatments are often used in ailments attributed to wind which collects in the body, to the corruption of the blood, and to eating foods which are hotter or colder than body temperature [Dow 1965:46–47; see also Métraux 1953:67]

Although Weidman (1978) makes it clear that Haitian immigrants in Miami continue to use folk medicine and to consult folk healers, their use of these modes of therapy is limited. Clarissa Scott points out (1974:527) that "medicinal preparations and elements of the traditional Haitian health care system are limited in Miami, possibly because their population is not yet large enough to support more than a handful of indigenous healers." Thus the size of the Haitian enclave affects reliance on traditional healers.

Sometimes the use of home remedies and folk healers leads to complications, because patients wait too long before they see a physician. Some patients, on the other hand, seek to enhance their chance of a cure by consulting a physician and a folk healer simultaneously.

Voodoo Healers

Voodooist folk healers are often voodoo priests who have had long training in the study of the spirit mythology and the properties of plants. Their treatments are based on prayers and herbal remedies, which were learned from elders in accordance with oral traditions. The transmission of folk medical knowledge from one generation to the next follows specific rules and is often learned during illness episodes.

Spiritual causation may be suspected and a voodoo practitioner consulted if symptoms recur at approximately the same time every day or if a child is born with a physical deformity. Ancestor spirits, as we have seen, are believed to cause illness if a descendant has not contributed toward the annual ceremonial meal in their honor. Physical deformities are more likely to be attributed to an angry spirit who has been enlisted by an enemy to perform an act of witchcraft. Many psychiatric disorders are also attributed to spiritual causes (Kiev 1961, 1962; Mathewson 1975).

Although these conditions are the typical reasons for consulting a voodoo priest, any very sick person is likely to be pressured by friends to see a voodoo healer. Sometimes voodoo priests themselves activate their networks of contacts to enlist sick clients. Furthermore, because illness may indicate a dereliction of filial duty, some Haitian-Americans are ashamed of being sick and believe that their friends will look down on them if they do not seek help from a voodoo healer. Thus in desperate situations, and in others when personalized treatment is wanted for little money, the sick are likely to turn to such healers.

Illnesses of supernatural origin are said to be cured only when proper rituals are performed to appease specific spirits and when the spirits' demands, as interpreted by a voodoo priest, are met. The spirit may make its intentions known in two ways: through ritual possession it may explain the nature of the illness and advise on the course of action to be taken; or it may manifest itself in a dream directly to the patient, explaining the nature of the illness, the ritual to be performed, and the herbal remedies to be taken (Laguerre 1980b).

The patient is required to play a more active role in traditional voodoo treatment than in modern medical settings. The patient "has to gather funds and may be required to purchase materials used in the treatment. Often there is a great deal of preparation involved. Furthermore, he receives sympathy and assurance from his family and friends. Since his illness creates a serious economic burden, there may be considerable pressure on him to return to his regular duties" (Dow 1965:50).

Other Caribbean healing traditions share some features of Haitian practices, among them the belief that interaction between humans and spirits is an important means of preventing illness and of regaining one's health. There is some evidence of cross-fertilization and syncretism among Mesa Blanca, santería, and voodoo in New York (see Garrison 1977, Harwood 1977). Haitians have introduced Cuban, Puerto Rican, and Dominican acquaintances to voodoo healers, and some Haitians have consulted Spanish-speaking healers. In both situations the patient relates to the healer through an interpreter. Weidman (1978:662) found that in Miami "at least one Bahamian and one southern black respondent mentioned involvement with a Haitian therapist. . . . Haitians are seeing local southern black therapists along with Bahamian and southern black clients."

Pharmacies

Licensed pharmacies that cater to Haitian-Americans stock the herbal remedies and other medications that their clients customarily bought in Haiti. Some markets and groceries in Haitian enclaves also carry the herbs that Haitians use to make teas and other home remedies.

Encounters with Mainstream Medical Practitioners

Settings for Medical Care

Haitians tend to seek medical care from Haitian physicians who have developed a good reputation on the island before migrating to the United States. Some people seek out a physician they have used previously in Haiti.

Most Haitian physicians are in general practice and serve a Haitian clientele. They report difficulty in collecting the fees due them, however, because of their patients' feeling that as they and the doctor are compatriots in a foreign land, their relationship should be a personal one, and payment would be inappropriate. This attitude has its roots in medical practices in Haiti, where physicians vary their fees in accordance with the patient's economic status and with any kinship ties that may exist between them. As a result of the difficulty over fees, some Haitian physicians prefer not to attract a Haitian clientele. For many illegal immigrants, however, Haitian physicians are the main sources of care (Weidman 1978:267).

A few Haitians use the services of Medicaid clinics. They are generally reluctant to do so, however, because free services are assumed to be inferior. In any case, Medicaid clinics are generally understaffed, and the likelihood of finding a Creole-speaking employee to act as interpreter is slim.

In general, Haitian-Americans consider hospitals to be the ultimate health-care resource centers, but they go to one only when they have become convinced that their self-diagnosis (made with the help of friends and relatives) is wrong. As one lower-class informant put it, "I have tried every single herbal remedy, and I still could not be cured. So I decided to go [to] the hospital." The particular hospital is chosen on the advice of associates who know which facilities have Haitian staff members.

After delaying medical care until they are in distress, Haitian-Americans frequently go to the emergency room of a hospital.[9] For them, "emergency" means that someone will take care of them when they get there; thus assurance of prompt treatment in other outpatient facilities would undoubtedly go far toward reducing use of the emergency room by Haitian patients.

The plight of the Haitian-American hospital patient is well illustrated in the following case, recounted by a Haitian nurse: A Haitian woman who suffered from back pain was unable either to sit down or to walk, and was confined to bed at home. Assuming that her problems would clear up in time, she made some "tea for gas" and awaited results. After two weeks or so with no improvement, however, she went to a hospital.

9. On the pattern of use of emergency rooms in U.S. hospitals by new immigrants, see Grossman 1976:130; see also McKinlay 1972.

There she passed through the regular business of registration and waiting. Finally, after a quick examination, she was sent to another hospital. The time she spent waiting did not match the short time she was with the physician. She was a bit frustrated to find that she had to start all over again at the second hospital, and was considerably upset when she was placed in a wheelchair. For this patient, as for many Haitian patients, the wheelchair is a sign of serious illness; to sit in one is to proclaim one's illness. Since in Haitian culture illness is to be shared only among family and friends, this public display of weakness arouses considerable emotion. In Haitian culture, too, illness must be accepted heroically. A person must be strong, for being psychologically weak is a way of letting illness dominate one's body.

The woman is a light-skinned member of a middle-class family in Queens, and her indignation grew with each question she was asked. Had she ever had syphilis? She was shocked; that is not the kind of question one asks a person from a distinguished Catholic family. She received a second blow when she was asked to take a test for sickle-cell anemia. In her mind, she is mulatto, not black. She has never identified herself as a black; why should she take a test for a condition associated with blacks? At the physician's insistence, however, she agreed to the test. Later she was relieved to learn that the result was negative.

She agreed to surgery because she had no alternative. She could not read or speak English. An interpreter brought a release for her signature. When she learned what she was being asked to sign—her agreement that the hospital could not be held liable should she die during the surgery—she became very frightened and emotional. The meaning of the release form was clear to her: the physician was incompetent and therefore she might die. She could not believe that the hospital would tell her that she might die and yet expect her to go through with the operation. Her experience in Haiti had taught her that surgeons were always very positive and helpful. This physician seemed to her to be far too pessimistic. In her view, pessimism was not a good attitude to take into an operating room. A Haitian nurse came to explain that her surgery was a routine procedure and that every patient was asked to sign a release. It did not mean that she was going to die. The surgery was performed without complications, and she spent a few more days in the hospital to recover.

In the days following her surgery, the woman's physician and nurses came to say hello and to compliment her on her progress. Yet their courtesy did not help her relations with them. Their visits upset her. The language barrier prevented her from thanking them for their kindness—if indeed they were being kind. Were their visits social or professional? Not understanding their language, she could never decipher their intentions.

As this account illustrates, surgery is greatly feared among Haitian-Americans, regardless of class. The possibility of death, however remote, cannot be ignored. The patient and relatives are therefore likely to become quite emotional and to require considerable reassurance.

Language Problems

The language problem in medical settings looms large for most Haitians. When Haitians are asked if they speak French, they almost invariably say they do, though in fact most of them do not, as we have seen. And so they are likely to be assigned a French-speaking physician, and communication problems persist.

As a result, most Haitians prefer to bring a family member or friend to interpret for them, especially as they are generally reluctant to let a stranger know about their problems. Women are particularly suspicious in this regard, fearing that an unknown interpreter may spread gossip in the community and cause them embarrassment; they may even avoid consulting a Haitian physician for fear that their problems may become known among other Haitians. Yet despite the desire to have a confidant act as interpreter, people are reluctant to ask a close associate to accompany them if the associate will have to miss work.

During a stay in the hospital the language problem becomes a particular source of stress. Although patients may have the assistance of interpreters in their interactions with physicians, most of the time they are left alone to communicate with the nurses and other hospital personnel as best they can. The language gap also leaves them isolated from their roommates and other patients with whom they would speak if they could.

English-speaking Haitians may also become upset when a physician does not allow them enough time to find the proper English words for an idea they wish to convey, and they have even greater difficulty in communicating if the physician shows exasperation over their manner of speaking. Furthermore, patients hesitate to ask questions if the physician seems rushed, even if they have not understood the physician's explanations.[10]

Physician-Patient Communication

When a physician tries to refer a Haitian patient to a specialist, the Haitian tends to go to a Haitian doctor, for three basic reasons: the language barrier, the belief that a Haitian physician is in a better position to understand the patient's financial problems, and a lack of familiarity with the distinction between specialists and general practitioners.

The dialogue between a physician and patient may also lead the patient to conclude that a visit to a voodoo healer is indicated. Such statements as "I can't tell what you have; I need more tests to find out"; "I'm not certain what the trouble is; I'm going to send you to another physician" may lead patients to suspect that their problems are caused by a supernatural agency, if even the physician cannot tell what is wrong.

Most American physicians do not ask their patients about the kinds of folk medication they have been taking, though they generally ask about prescribed medications. Patients are thus led to believe that they need not concern themselves with any possible conflict between their home remedies and the medications or diets the physician prescribes. A physician who deals with such ethnic patients as Haitians, who take herbal and over-the-counter medications routinely and quite pervasively, should make some inquiry into the nature of home remedies in order to determine if in fact any are contraindicated.

Haitian patients may be able to provide only vague descriptions of their illnesses as symptoms tend to be defined imprecisely. The

10. Julian Samora and his colleagues (1966:293) have pointed out that "a generalized complaint by patients [was] that they did not understand much of what physicians told them and that matters pertaining to the illness and its course were not explained to them in terms they could understand."

ability to specify the site of pain, for example, depends on one's concept of illness. In the view of many Haitians, when a person is ill, the entire body is ill. Thus the causes of pain are not necessarily located at the site of the pain itself, and the location of pain is consequently of little importance, especially as pain is believed to shift from one location to another.

The Haitian pattern of verbal communication tends to make considerable use of metaphoric and symbolic language, which complicates cross-cultural communication (Laguerre 1970). Euphemisms are commonly used for body parts and for stigmatized diseases and symptoms: *ti pijon* ("my pigeon") for penis, *maladi tonbé* ("the illness that makes you fall down") for epilepsy. The patient may also be reticent for fear of making a mistake. The physician interacting with a Haitian patient may consequently have difficulty discovering exactly what the problem is. Both patient and physician become frustrated as the physician repeatedly asks questions that the patient believes have already been clearly answered. Such difficulties may well lead the patient to return to a folk practitioner for care.

In general, Haitian patients tend to tell their physicians what illness they think they have, instead of describing or explaining their symptoms. Most Haitian patients consult physicians not to find out the cause of their discomfort but to get help for the illness they have already diagnosed. Health is considered to be a personal responsibility, and one therefore needs to be able to diagnose oneself. When patients describe their symptoms, they tend to emphasize the ones that they think correspond to the diseases they have in mind. What health professionals hear is thus not necessarily a description of felt symptoms but their patients' interpretations of the facts to corroborate their own diagnoses.

Educated Haitian migrants tend to use familiar biomedical disease labels. Such specific terms as malaria, *tension* (a Creole word for both hypotension and hypertension), *poitrinaire* (tuberculosis), diabetes, and rheumatism are sometimes used by poorly educated migrants as well, but often with meanings different from those assigned by biomedical professionals. Usually these concepts were learned when, at the insistence of a patient or the patient's family, the physician has named the patient's disease but has not explained its nature or how the disease process relates to the symptoms. As a result, people may use a biomedical term that does not correspond to their own symptoms.

Expectations in the Medical Encounter

Haitian patients generally want a quick diagnosis, and they want to be treated politely. They want to be able to believe that their physicians are as interested in helping them as in making money.

Physicians who fail to use their stethoscopes are likely to be considered incompetent. So are doctors who let a patient leave without a prescription. And many lower-class Haitians are convinced that an expensive prescription is better than an inexpensive one.

Adherence to Physicians' Recommendations

Haitian-Americans' adherence to the course of treatment prescribed for them depends to a great extent on their perception of the graveness of the illness and on their socioeconomic and legal status. An illness is considered to be grave when it has caused the death of a member of the family or a friend, or when the physician tells the patient it is. Such patients generally do their best to follow the physician's recommendations. Certain diseases—cancer, heart disease, diabetes—are generally regarded as grave in and of themselves. Patients who do not consider their illness grave and do not fear the outcome take a more relaxed stance toward treatment. Fear of an illness does not prevent a Haitian from taking home remedies, however. Although home remedies may be classified as "hot" and "cold," according to folk concepts, prescription medicines are not.

In general, Haitian patients have difficulty following dietary restrictions. Diabetics in particular have problems when they come to this country, because they often do not know which of the many new foods they encounter in the United States are safe for them. Work restrictions are also particularly hard for Haitians to follow, since many have come to this country specifically to make money.

Although many Haitians buy life insurance policies, few buy

health insurance, and they are frequently unaware of the various forms of disability insurance available to them through their jobs. Even when Haitian migrants have insurance, many are afraid to use it too often for fear of exceeding the amount of money they believe they are entitled to, and many are unable to fill out the proper forms for reimbursement. As a result, a large number of Haitians return to work after a hospital stay sooner than their doctors have advised, because they must support themselves and pay their drug and other medical bills.

Undocumented Haitians face particularly critical problems in receiving adequate health care from hospitals. They tend to give false names in order to maintain their anonymity and to change hospitals and physicians often; the physician is therefore unable to get in touch with the patient for follow-up care, or to obtain medical records from other hospitals or physicians.

Recovery, Rehabilitation, and Death

When Haitian patients are discharged from a hospital, relatives or friends pick them up and take them home. People with chronic incapacitating illnesses are usually cared for at home by their families; they are unlikely to be placed in nursing homes.

Rituals associated with the resumption of one's normal roles after an illness are often linked to promises one has made to supernatural beings during one's stay in the hospital. After a grave illness Catholic patients may pay for a mass of thanksgiving or make a pilgrimage to a shrine in the United States, Canada, or Haiti. Voodoo believers, as well, may perform a special voodoo ceremony to thank the spirits for their recovery.

Death always mobilizes the entire extended family. Funeral arrangements are usually made by a male kinsman of the deceased who, because of his education and fluency in English, has had experience in dealing with American bureaucracies. Such a person should preferably be the deceased's oldest son.

Ethnicity and Health Care

The health behaviors of Haitian-Americans suggest that there is an interplay between ethnicity and health care. The immigrants' health habits, reflecting their past socialization in traditional Haitian culture, are strongly tied to the use of folk medicine.

The notion of dependent ethnicity can best be understood in the medical domain because it is there that ethnic minorities tend to experience most keenly the feeling of being in a culturally subordinate position. By "dependent ethnicity" I mean the process by which an ethnic culture comes to interact in a subordinate way with a majority or national culture. Dependent ethnicity may be experienced whenever a patient from an ethnic subculture has an encounter with the medical staff of a modern hospital. Ethnic patients often have their own way of understanding and coping with illness, and medical personnel seldom pay attention to their views. Nurses, physicians, dietitians, and laboratory professionals have all, as Rachel Spector (1979:78) puts it, been "socialized into the culture of their profession."

The provider culture has its own ways of providing health care. The modern hospital can be considered a total institution in which administrative personnel, medical staff, and patients are subjected to formal and informal rules that regulate their behaviors (see Goffman 1961). The ethnic patient must adhere to the rules of the provider culture. Often the lack of flexibility of medical personnel causes a breakdown in the communication process between the professional health provider and the ethnic patient (Samora, Saunders, and Larson 1966).

Other investigators have found wide variations in reactions to pain (Zborowski 1952), compliance with medical recommendations (Becker et al. 1975), and illness behaviors (Zola 1964) among and within ethnic groups. Such variables as income, educational attainment, and religious affiliation influence behavior quite as much as ethnicity (Harwood, ed., 1981; Jackson 1981). Indeed, class variations in the health-seeking behaviors of Haitian-Americans have also been observed. The majority of Haitian-Americans, however, live in slum districts and have the diseases and illnesses prevalent among ghetto residents. Poverty and membership in a low-status ethnic minority are two important factors that prevent them from benefiting from the American medical system (Bullough and Bullough 1972:5). The public hospitals that the majority of Haitian-Americans use are generally overcrowded and understaffed, and the physicians the patients encounter there are likely to be in training. One cannot say that these hospitals are equipped to give adequate care to immigrants who are members of low-status ethnic minorities.

[7]

Political Life

In the early 1960s the international press identified New York City as the bastion of Haitian-American opposition to François Duvalier's administration (Ledur 1973, Cando and Jorge 1966). The explanation for such active political involvement by émigrés lies in the fact that most of the Haitian immigrants in the city at that time had performed some governmental function under the five presidents who had held office during 1956 and 1957. Since the independence of the island in 1804, Haitian government leaders have always given state jobs to their supporters as a kind of political payoff. François Duvalier was no exception to that policy. Each new wave of patronage left a backwash of former employees who were ready to join the ranks of the opposition. Most of the émigrés in the 1960s still had families and properties in Haiti and were organizing to overthrow Papa Doc. They still hope to return to the island someday (Laguerre 1980a).

More than thirty political groups, whose main reason for existence has been the hoped-for overthrow of the two Duvalier regimes, have functioned in New York City since 1957. Some have operated clandestinely and have made their existence known by leaflets, pamphlets, and occasional newspapers distributed in the community. Their secrecy, based on fear of reprisals against family members still living in Haiti (Thompson 1972), makes an analysis of their operations before 1971 difficult. From 1971 on, however, with the death of Papa Doc and the seeming liberalization of the administration of Jean-Claude Duvalier, most groups have come into the open (Jumelle 1973).

Despite such problems, no study of the Haitian immigrant community in New York City can ignore the participation of such groups in local-level politics. Ethnic politics is at the center of the lives of a considerable segment of the Haitian-American population in New York.[1] Their political activities have played a large part in the integration of the Haitian-American community into the mainstream of American society.

The Evolution of Haitian-American Politics in New York City

Haitian-American politics is structured within the particular socioeconomic circumstances in which it has evolved. It is shaped within a structure of inequality and dependence intrinsic to the very nature of American society as a capitalist nation.[2] The early immigrants, mostly from the Haitian upper class, were unable to maintain their elite status in the United States for many reasons, not least the racial ideology that permeates every aspect of American life and culture. Haitian-American politics has evolved in response to these structural societal constraints. This response, however, has not been univocal; immigrants have followed various adaptive patterns in respect to participation in political activities. The Haitian-American political parties in New York are class-based entities.

The evolution of Haitian-American politics in New York reflects the history of Haitian emigration, as various waves of immigrants have added ingredients to the stew of Haitian-American politics. Three distinct phases of Haitian-American political activities in New York can be identified, each related to a phase of Haitian emigration: the phase of invasions, 1956–64; the phase of the right-wing coalition, 1965–70; and the phase of the explosion of presidential candidates, leftist groups, and the beginning of a progressivist coalition, 1971–77 (Laguerre 1980a).

In the first phase, former presidents, presidential candidates, and their families and supporters were followed to New York by

1. Buchanan 1980 and Glick 1975 provide analyses of Haitian politics in New York City from a different perspective.

2. George De Vos (1980) has done much to clarify our understanding of the psychological adaptation of immigrant minorities.

some army officers and their families and by Duvalier followers who had fallen into disgrace because of the political activities of their relatives abroad. In the second phase, professionals, students, and other people who belonged to associations that were declared illegal left the island in large numbers. The third phase is the result of chain migration (MacDonald and MacDonald 1964, Graves and Graves 1974), as people in New York sent for their families and friends to join them (Laguerre 1978a, 1978c). Since 1971, both city dwellers and peasants have been coming to New York and Florida either through legal channels or as boat people (Segal 1975, Souffrant 1974).

Invasions, 1956–64

The Haitian elite who came to the United States from 1956 to 1964 had to face the hard reality of racial discrimination. Having been members of the upper class in Haiti, they now found themselves members of the most despised racial group in American society, and their incomes had been left behind. "Because of the need to migrate at any cost, most Haitians, irrespective of their social class, background, previous work experience, or level of education, were willing to accept the first job they were offered" (Dominguez 1975:42). As we shall see, whether they had espoused a democratic, technocratic, or populist political philosophy, their vision of the political reforms needed in Haiti was shaped by their reading of the American political system and the prospect of their eventual return to Haiti.

From 1956 to 1964 the Haitian-American political scene in New York was dominated by traditional politicians, men who had been either presidents, army officers, or cabinet members. These right-wing politicians agreed on a certain number of principles. First, they needed a presidential candidate. Second, they wished to introduce some reforms, not radical changes, to the Haitian governmental system. One major reform goal was an increase in legislative power at the expense of the executive branch. They agreed to reduce political repression by giving amnesty to political prisoners and by permitting freedom of the press and of speech (*En Avant*, July 1975). They were also willing, according to some informants, to work with the CIA, which would provide them with a military camp in which to train guerrillas who would launch invasions of Haiti.

Men who supported a return to traditional democracy in Haiti grouped themselves around former president Paul-Eugène Magloire. The Magloire group played a central role in the opposition. Magloire was the leader most talked about because it was believed that he helped to finance some of the invasions and because many émigrés saw in him the messiah who would save the nation. His years as president of Haiti, from 1950 to 1956, gave him prestige, and some people believed that he was supported by the U.S. State Department. The Magloire group, which had alliances with army officers in Haiti, launched several invasions of the island, all of which failed. The group's main strategy was to be faithful to State Department policies in regard to Haiti and to ask the CIA to help train some of their men in guerrilla warfare (Jumelle 1973). As most of the groups needed to claim that they had CIA support in order to attract followers, it is difficult to determine to what extent the CIA did in fact help them. The Magloire group was credited with the launching of the most important invasion of the island. On July 29, 1958, a group of former army officers and a few American mercenaries occupied the Casernes Dessalines, the army headquarters in Port-au-Prince, and kept the presidential guards occupied for four hours (Diederich and Burt 1964). The invaders were all killed by late afternoon (Bodson, Ripet, and Lefèvre 1970:62; Saintil 1966:96).

Not all politicians subscribed to the Magloire group's ideology. Some believed that economic progress could be achieved in Haiti only through the establishment of a technocratic democracy, and formed their own political party. Their main goal was to replace the Duvalier government by a team of competent administrators, a group of technocrats who had shown intellectual and administrative skills as professionals and who were to lead the country to prosperity through the development of peripheral capitalism. Le Parti Social Chrétien, led by Père George, and Jeune Haïti, led by Père Bissainthe, both representatives of the technocratic political philosophy, also attempted a few invasions of the island. Thirteen young men lost their lives in a 1964 invasion sponsored by Jeune Haïti (Cando and Jorge 1966:76). Two of them were captured, taken to Port-au-Prince, and executed for high treason; the others were killed during a confrontation with the armed forces. Two other technocratically oriented political parties, the Union Démocratique Nationale (UDN) and the Mouvement Révolutionnaire Haïtien (MRH), also recruited members in New York during this period (Jumelle 1973:40). The traditional and technocratic democrats were primarily of the middle and upper classes; lower-class Haitian immigrants interested in opposition politics were to be found among the populist democrats.

The Mouvement d'Organisation du Pays (MOP), a populist group, has a good number of followers among low-income Haitian-Americans in Brooklyn, the home of its leader, Daniel Fignolé, who was a provisional president of Haiti for nineteen days in 1957. Fignolé, who migrated in 1957, is one of the rare opposition leaders who has stayed among the lower-class people who formed his constituency in Haiti. The MOP disseminates its party instructions through *Construction*, a bimonthly newsletter.

The Right-Wing Coalition, 1965–70

The organization of Haitian-American politics in New York bears the imprint of the institutional and structural crises that the United States underwent in the late 1960s. The civil rights movement was then at its peak and the Vietnam war was taking its toll of Haitian-American lives. It was in these circumstances, when Haitian immigrants looked back to Haiti as the promised land, that the Haitian-American Coalition was formed.

The Coalition Haïtienne, composed of Jeune Haïti, Les Forces Révolutionnaires Haïtiennes (FRH), Le Mouvement Révolutionnaire du 12 Novembre (MR 12 Novembre), and followers of Magloire, was formed in 1964, the year that François Duvalier was elected president for life. The opposition decided that it was time for unity of action if the island was ever to be rid of Duvalier. With the exception of the MOP, all of the other groups mentioned earlier also participated in the coalition activities. They published a weekly newsletter, *Le Combattant Haï-*

tien, and broadcast messages to Haiti on Radio Vonvon in a vain attempt to incite the Haitian people to revolt against Duvalier. During this period Magloire remained the undisputed leader of the coalition. The coalition was credited with the bombing of the National Palace in June 1969 (Bodson, Ripet, and Lefèvre 1970). Two old planes had taken off from the Bahamas, but mechanical problems prevented one of the planes from delivering its cargo of bombs.

Division within the coalition and rivalry with other opposition groups undermined its effectiveness. More and more of its efforts were diverted from the overthrow of Duvalier to the formulation of responses to its critics. The following reply, for example, was directed to Haitian émigrés in Cuba, who were using Radio Havana to send political messages to Haiti critical of the coalition's counterrevolutionary politics:

> Radio Havana maintains that the Haitian coalition is giving sleeping pills to the Haitian people through its Radio broadcast originating in New York City over Radio New York worldwide. Duvalier characterizes the radio broadcasting from the territory of a member country of the OAS as 'a main threat' to his regime of terror. Thus Dictator Duvalier has ordered the jamming of the Radio signals of 'La Voie de l'Union', that is, of the democratic voice. Radio Havana considers itself revolutionary and anti-imperialist, meaning anti-American, yet Duvalier does not interfere with the signals of Radio Havana. What are we to conclude? [*Combattant Haïtien*, March 8, 1968]

The Haitian Coalition was dismantled in early 1970 to form La Résistance Haïtienne. In January 1970 this group organized a public demonstration in the United Nations Plaza in an attempt to prevent Papa Doc from nominating his son Jean-Claude as his successor. To achieve this goal, even Communist partisans joined the new group, as did a group of coast guardsmen who had rebelled against the Duvalier administration and had been granted refugee status in the United States. The presence of Communist elements in La Résistance provoked internal conflicts, and the group slowly dissolved. A few individual members, however, have continued the struggle through the publication of the opposition newspaper *Haïti Observateur*.

Presidential Candidates and Leftist Groups, 1971–77

In times of crisis an ethnic group may achieve cohesion if it feels that outside forces are threatening its membership. Here may lie the explanation for the coalition's momentum during the Vietnam era. With the death of Papa Doc and the end of the Vietnam war, however, the coalition split into several political parties, each backing its own presidential candidate, and Marxist groups flourished.

By the time Duvalier died, on April 21, 1971, Magloire's coalition force had lost its momentum. With the repeated failures of the invasions that he helped finance, his support waned, and several potential leaders pressed forward to fill the vacuum at the top during the first two years of Jean-Claude Duvalier's administration. Some succeeded in transmitting their political vision to a good number of followers; others managed to convince only their relatives and friends.

The best known of the candidates was Antoine Colas, a Haitian professional, who had lived in Africa. Sometime in June 1971, Colas, unknown until then, organized a mass meeting at which he announced that he was about to return to Haiti to replace Baby Doc. The State Department and Aristotle Onassis, he proclaimed, were ready to finance the coup. According to Colas, the American government was working with the Haitian army to force Duvalier out of office and replace him with Colas. In all of his public appearances, he was carefully protected by bodyguards. He set a date to leave for Haiti, and on the day of his departure several newsmen came to accompany him. He went to Haiti, met with a few government officials, and after three days returned to New York. Since then he has made no public appearances.

During the summer of 1971 another leader, Henry Vixamar, emerged. He, too, claimed to be backed by the American government. He had earlier worked for the Chad government, and he assured the New York Haitian community that Chad and other African countries were about to finance his project to replace Duvalier. Vixamar used the pages of *Réalités Haïtiennes* to spell out the major points of his political program, stressing the need to restore political freedom in Haiti and to bring the nation to economic prosperity and stability. While in exile in New York, he declared himself the undisputed leader of the Haitian Revolutionary Forces and the supreme chief of the army. After a few months of making headlines in New York, he withdrew from public life.

Two other leaders previously unknown in the Haitian-American community also emerged during the summer of 1971. Emmanuel Fordes assured the public that some African governments were helping him to overthrow Duvalier, and Dr. Ernest Fénélon, a Vietnam veteran, claimed that the State Department had been impressed by his work in Vietnam and wanted to help out. At public appearances in New York and Chicago Fénélon talked about correspondence with Senator Edward Kennedy on the matter and announced that some of his men were being trained in guerrilla warfare under CIA supervision. None of these self-proclaimed candidates achieved the momentum of Antoine Colas.

From 1971 on, leftist political groups have proliferated in the New York Haitian-American community. Marxist-Leninist, Marxist-Maoist, and progressivist socialist coalitions hold meetings open to the public but at this writing none has put forward a presidential candidate.

The Marxist-Leninist and Marxist-Maoist groups have very few members, most of them no more than four or five. The leftist intellectuals who form them have a great capacity for political literary production. Their newspapers and other occasional publications show more familiarity with standard Marxist thought than with Haitian empirical reality. As the Haiti of the Duvaliers has received very little authoritative attention and as Haitian Marxists have not been able to return to the island, they tend to get their basic information on Haiti from the international press and the literary productions of their colleagues—works filled with revolutionary slogans and political rhetoric but with little systematic analysis of the current Haitian situation.

The two militant leftist groups in New York, the Voie Démocratique (Marxist-Leninist) and the Rassemblement des Forces Démocratiques (Marxist-Maoist), stand firm on anti-Duvalier and anti-imperialist principles. Though they do not offer presidential candidates, they look to a few individuals as the only ones capable of interpreting the writings of Marx, Lenin, and Mao. In the words of an informant, the leftist politicians present themselves first as Maoist or Leninist and second as Haitian (see also Laraque n.d.:5).

Other political activists opposed to both Duvalier and Magloire group themselves in various ways to bring about structural changes in Haiti. All subscribe to an eventual socialist revolution. In mid-1971 the progressivist forces—Heure Haïtienne, Troupe Kouidor, Brigade Gerald Baker, Club Mappou, and the Mouvement 2ème Indépendance—regrouped to form the Comité de Mobilisation (Ledur 1973:9; *Réalités Haitiennes*, June 6, 1971). It soon fell apart as a result of internal conflicts. Another effort to regroup the progressivist forces was made after a public demonstration against Duvalier in front of the Haitian Consulate in New York on July 28, 1971. The Mouvement Haïtien d'Action Patriotique (MHAP) was formed during this period to bring together Haitians with seemingly nonconflicting ideologies who were willing to support anti-imperialist and antiopportunist revolutionary movements inside Haiti (*Patriote Haïtien*, February 8, 1973).

In February 1972 the Rassemblement des Forces Progressistes Haïtiennes was formed of Réalités Haïtiennes, which published the newspaper of the same name; Le Rassemblement Démocratique Haïtien (RDH); and the Organisation Révolutionnaire du 12 Novembre (OR 12 Novembre). Another coalition, KODDPA (Komité kap Défann Doua pèp Ayisyin, or Committee for the Defense of Human Rights in Haiti), was formed later. KODDPA has lobbied in Washington on behalf of the Miami refugees and in 1977 brought a successful suit in federal court to secure the release of imprisoned refugees. Human rights violations in Haiti have also received KODDPA's attention.

On May 17–18 and August 30–31, 1975, the Equipe des Prêtres de la Revue Sel, the Inion Fanm Ayisyin Patriot (IFAP), the Mouvement du 22 Août, the Mouvement Haïtien d'Action Patriotique (MHAP), and the Rassemblement des Forces Progressistes Haïtiennes (RFPH) met to write the constitution underlying the formation of the Comité pour le Regroupement des Forces Démocratiques Haïtiennes (CRFDH) (*Patriote Haitien*, January 6, 1976). By 1977 the following New York groups held membership in the organization: the Forces Armées Révolutionnaires Haïtiennes (FARH), the Mouvement du 22 Août, the Rassemblement des Forces Patriotiques Haïtiennes (RFPH), and the Patriotes

Indépendants (*Patriote Haitien*, March 18, 1977). Their goal is to form a solid core of Haitian democratic forces in exile in order to study the conditions that make it possible for the Duvaliers to remain so long in office, to overthrow Jean-Claude Duvalier, and to propose and implement democratic policies for the well-being of the nation (*Patriote Haitien*, April 7, 1977).

Haitian Participation in American Politics

If the Vietnam war, institutional racism, and the civil rights movement induced some Haitian émigrés to look back to Haiti as the promised land, they inspired others to participate in the American political process. Those who fought in the civil rights movement became convinced that their goals could be achieved only in the American political arena.

Indeed, a growing number of Haitian-American politicians have been engaged in American politics. They are found mainly among the educated middle class and especially among Haitian immigrants who arrived in the city before 1956. They came for economic reasons and intended to stay here for the rest of their lives. They have American citizenship and were partly educated in New York universities and professional schools. Others who came later also had intended to make careers in North America.

In 1968 a group of Haitian-Americans met to form the Haitian-American Political Organization. Until then no political group in New York had lobbied on behalf of the Haitian-American community, though "members of the Haitian population had been in contact with American political campaigns on several occasions. However, none of these earlier contacts materialized into any sustained group activity. They lent prestige to individuals within the population" (Glick 1975:256).

During the presidential campaigns of 1968 the leaders of the Haitian-American Political Organization were invited to Washington to attend meetings of leaders of ethnic communities organized by the Democratic party. The organization immediately acquired some national visibility. The association's leaders worked very actively as volunteers for the Humphrey-Muskie campaign in 1968, in the process acquiring political experience and broadening their contacts among New York politicians. At that time the leaders were "interested in building the Haitian political organization so that it would be large enough and strong enough to act as an interest group for the Haitian population" (Glick 1975:290; see also Schiller 1977).

The Haitian-American Political Organization is the manifestation of the community's interest in being a part of the political and decision-making process in America. It helps to make the Haitian presence felt as a political force and makes Haitian-Americans aware of the possibilities of negotiating their votes for public services to be provided to the community.

In 1971 Max Laudun, a member of the Haitian-American Citizens Society and chairman of the Haitian-American Liberal Party Club of Queens County, was the official candidate of the Liberal party for a seat in the New York State Assembly (20th district). He gained 2,421 votes against his Republican opponent, who won with 13,400 votes.

One year later, in 1972, Louis A. Brun was invited by Senator Waldaba Stewart, New York State convener, to be a member of the New York State delegation to the National Black Political Convention, held on March 10–12 in Gary, Indiana. Brun was also a candidate for the State Assembly (53d district) and was the official candidate of the International Reformed Democratic Club. He, too, was defeated.

In 1975 the Haitian-American Registered Voters Equality Service Team (HARVEST) used the columns of the local newspaper *Unité* to urge Haitian-Americans to vote in the forthcoming presidential election. In New York's mayoral campaign in 1977, Haitian-Americans supported black candidate Percy E. Sutton, Manhattan borough president. Sutton named Brun as chairman of his "election committee on the nationalities," which was to engage in "recruiting and coordinating the electoral activities of the various ethnic groups which are supporting the candidacy of Mr. Sutton for mayor of New York City" (*Unité*, January 15, 1977).

The participation of Haitian immigrants in American politics is shaped by structural constraints imposed on the ethnic community and by the adaptive strategies developed by the community to improve its lot. It therefore reflects, on the one hand, the external conditions that maintain the boundaries of the ethnic group, and on the other, the subculture in which it is expressed.

Ethnicity and Political Culture

Politics often serves as a cohesive factor in the development of ethnic consciousness.[3] It can be used to reinforce the emotional awareness of ethnic membership, especially when the interests of the group appear to be threatened. The Haitian-American Political Organization, for example, was created for the purpose of sensitizing Haitian-American voters to the need to organize themselves into a pressure group in order to improve the services provided to their neighborhoods. Politics can also foster group divisions, especially when individual members adhere to conflicting ideologies. Ideological differences can polarize an ethnic community, as we have seen. Ethnic politics provides political alternatives among which individuals must choose.

The division of the Haitian-American opposition, with its various competing political groups, clearly suggests the possibility that class consciousness can be used to rally individuals behind various political ideologies. The class divisions in the New York Haitian-American population account for the variations in the manifestation of Haitian-American ethnicity. We have seen, for example, that members of the Haitian upper class rallied behind Magloire and the lower class behind Fignolé, while members of the educated middle class formed various Marxist-oriented groups. The symbolic content of urban ethnicity varies with the context of relational interactions, and the politics of an urban ethnic group also varies with the class positions and ideological options of its members.

Despite class and ideological differences, the Haitian-American community has been able to develop its own political culture. The creation of this culture was a result of three specific structural factors. First, the politically active members of the community have focused much of their attention on the political situation on the island, thus helping the community to maintain interest in the political groups abroad. Second, unable to return to the island, they have used multiple adaptive strategies to develop their own niche within the New York social landscape. Third, their political cul-

3. An evaluation of the various uses of the concept of ethnicity in the anthropological literature can be found in R. Cohen 1978. Valuable reviews of the literature on ethnicity, symbolism, and politics are provided by Vincent 1978 and A. Cohen 1979.

ture reflects their marginality and dependence on mainstream American society. Cultural encapsulation due to a dependency situation tends to foster the development of an ethnic subculture that reflects its structural position in the national political economy.

It is within the framework of this political culture that one needs to understand the emergence of several literary, folkloric, and musical groups, such as the Artistes Indépendants, the Troupe Kouidor, and Tanbou Libèté, whose public performances always deliver a political message. Nationalist and revolutionary songs have accompanied political opposition throughout the history of Haiti (Laguerre 1976).

In the New York niche, Haitian-Americans have developed a political vocabulary of their own to refer to the Haitian situation and to the reactionary politics of their opponents. Such Creole terms as *péi malouk* ("the country is in a big mess," for underdeveloped nation), *gro zoazo méchan* (predatory birds, for employees of the Duvalier government), and *bonbonflé* (fat little parasite, for Jean-Claude Duvalier) are given new political meanings. Haitian-Americans who live outside New York City are unlikely to be able to decode such terms.

Haitian immigrants have developed and maintained their political culture through the manipulation of certain symbols and rituals. Political and nationalist meetings have become cyclical rituals, whose main functions are to idealize the future and strengthen the ties among the political émigrés. Nationalist meetings are held on the anniversaries of historical events, such as the death of Dessalines and the Battle of Vertières. They all follow the same ritualistic pattern, beginning with the presentation of a presidential candidate or other leader. Then the speaker offers a negative critique of the Duvalier administration, giving the numbers of Haitians killed and imprisoned since 1957. He promises to restore peace and prosperity in Haiti and tells about his connection (or lack of it) with the U.S. State Department. He may finally ask other groups to join his, in order to form a united front. At this stage the master of ceremonies may ask the guests to help defray the expenses while collection baskets are passed. The meeting ends with the singing of the *Dessalinienne*, the Haitian national anthem.

The development of a political culture has not helped to diffuse the class alignments of the various political factions.[4] It has, however, provided a cultural context in which the interplay between class and ethnicity can be understood. Class ideology is an important variable to consider in attempting to reach an understanding of ethnic politics: in the ethnic political arena, class alliances and conflicts become manifest.

In the early 1960s, a good many Haitian-American immigrants took an interest in Haitian politics because they had been politically active in Haiti. By 1971, when Jean-Claude Duvalier was named president for life, some of these immigrants had become well settled in New York with well-paid jobs, and their interest in opposition politics had waned as they became increasingly integrated with American society. Haitian political organizations geared toward participation in the American political process, however, are still in an embryonic state.

Because of their perception and internalization of a dependency situation, Haitian-Americans have felt it necessary to use their ethnicity as an alternative way of maintaining or upgrading their class position. Dependence, while informing class consciousness, sets limits to the number of alternatives available for the manipulation of ethnicity. In a situation of asymmetric class relationships, ethnicity becomes the cultural imperative and often veils aspects of the pluralistic structure of dependence in an urban polyethnic environment.

In a dependency situation, ethnicity is used strategically by individuals and interest groups to improve their class-status position. Class interest is defined not by ethnicity but by economic viability structures within the limits of which ethnicity can be used as a strategic element for individual and group maneuvering. As Orlando Patterson puts it (1975:305; see also 1977:101), "ethnic loyalties reflect, and are maintained by, the underlying socio-economic interests of group members."

4. In a discussion of the problems confronted by minority groups, Louis Wirth has written (1972:147): "No ethnic group is ever unanimous in all of its attitudes and actions, and minority groups are no exception. They, too, have their internal differentiations, their factions and ideological currents and movements." For a discussion of ethnicity and politics in American society, see Fuchs 1968.

[8]

The World of the Immigrants

It has become evident throughout this study that the formation and maintenance of ethnic boundaries play a large part in Haitian-Americans' adaptation to and integration in American society. This observation seems to confirm Fredrik Barth's assertion (1969:15) that "the critical focus of investigation . . . becomes the ethnic boundary that defines the group, not the cultural stuff that it encloses." The Haitian immigrants make no conscious decision to form an ethnic group; the racist structure of American society compels them to use ethnicity in their adaptation process. As Andrew Greeley puts it (1976:8), "immigrants did not arrive as ethnics; they became such on the shores of their new country."

Haitian-Americans do not evolve in a world of their own, but in one in which racial discrimination and other forms of social inequality exist. Therefore, it is not enough to look at the cultural content of the ethnic group; equally important are the linkages and structural constraints in which the ethnic culture develops. For the cultural content cannot be understood except as a response or adaptation to an external reality (see Gans 1979:15). Haitian-American culture is in large part a response to developments in and interactions with the wider society.

The social position of racial minority groups can by no means be explained only in terms of their cultural orientation, as Ulf Hannerz (1974:56) seems to imply in the case of Afro-American ethnicity; more important are the ways in which blacks and other minorities have been treated (see also Mullings 1978). Their low status in the system indicates not a failure to devise strategies to improve their condition but rather intense pressures from the wider society to which they must adapt (see Vrga 1971:43). Because of these pressures, the experiences of racial minority groups cannot be equated with those of white ethnic groups in America.

Despite the divergent cultural and ideological orientations of immigrants to the United States, they all seem to share some similarities. For Oscar Handlin (1951:4), "the history of immigration is a history of alienation and its consequences." Most immigrants, whether black or white, tend to experience multiple miseries during the resettlement and adaptation process. They also share the will to improve their lot and that of their children. Black and white immigrants, however, have not fared equally in their pursuit of economic opportunity. The racial barrier adds a dimension to the everyday problems immigrants usually face. Skin color suddenly becomes a problem, and one that cannot be overcome. European immigrants who had to start life in America at the bottom of the socioeconomic ladder knew that their children, at least, had a realistic hope of improving their situation; even economic improvement does not solve the black immigrant's problem. Whether an intellectual, a bourgeois, or a beggar, the Haitian-American remains black.

It is often argued that all immigrants generally start at the bottom and over the years are able to improve their economic situations. But this is not always true. The stigmatization of some immigrant groups has made their adaptation more severe than that of others. "The Chinese were the first people whose presence was interdicted by exclusion acts. The Japanese were the one group declared an internal enemy and rounded up in concentration camps" (Blauner 1972:70). The belief that "all Americans started at the bottom" is indeed a fallacy. As Robert Blauner points out (1972:251), "the racial labor principle has meant in effect that 'the bottom' has by no means been the same for all groups."

The proposition that immigrants improve their lives with time is not always true, either. Many immigrants are caught in poverty for life (Fitzpatrick 1971:5–11). The structure of American society does not make it at all easy for minority racial groups to improve their lives; rather it often leads them to permanent niches in preexisting ethnic ghettos and pockets of poverty. Like most European immigrants, West Indian immigrants tend to settle in lower-class neighborhoods, but the difference between poor white and poor black neighborhoods is vast, and racial segregation withers the West Indians' hope of moving to a residential area of their choice.

Any comparison of West Indian immigrants with native-born black Americans is likely to be biased in several respects. Before the recent influx of Cuban and Haitian refugees, West Indian migration was selective. Mostly educated, young, and aggressive people came here with the intent of making money. The wider society's perception of them as foreign (read "exotic") enabled them to manipulate their ethnicity to their advantage. The ambiguity of the situation of more recent black immigrants is obvious. They are perceived as blacks by the wider society and are relegated to the same racial status as that of black Americans (see also Bryce-Laporte 1972). They consider themselves Haitians, Jamaicans, Trinidadians, and the like. Black Americans lump them all together as foreigners, though in Harlem, Haitians are often singled out as "French fries."[1] In the context of these perceptions, West Indian immigrants develop adaptive strategies to improve their opportunities and achieve upward mobility. They introduce themselves as West Indians in interactions with whites, for example, but identify themselves as blacks when they run for political office. As Thomas Sowell has pointed out (1975:148), West Indian immigrants "have gained political power largely as representatives of the black community as a whole." The appearance of more Haitian candidates in districts with large Haitian populations would enable the community to bargain from a position of strength.

The Haitian-American experience has demonstrated that ethnicity must be understood in its situational context, that is, the ecological and historical circumstances that help explain ethnic awareness. Ethnicity is used in a tactical manner to maintain and protect individual and group interests.[2] In the Haitian-American case, it is used as a response to a situation of dependency. Each ethnic identity taken by the immigrants (black, West Indian, Hai-

1. On the relationships between black Americans and West Indian immigrants, see Osofsky 1966, Cruse 1967, Raphael 1964, Spurling 1962.

2. A. L. Epstein speaks also (1978:xi) of "the affective dimension" of ethnicity and of "the powerful emotional charge that appears to surround or underlie so much of ethnic behavior."

tian) is manipulated in the context of their minority status in a white-dominated society. Their dependency situation obliges them to use their ethnicity as a means of survival. The awareness of such a situation is but one factor in ethnic consciousness. Haitian-Americans' consciousness of their dependency arises in large part with their passage from majority status in Haiti to minority status in the United States.

The Haitian-American community has emerged as an ethnic group because of external forces impinging on it and because of the ability of individuals to organize for their survival. Individuals have recognized the necessity to organize in order to enable their community to benefit from services offered by the city. State and local agencies are becoming increasingly aware of Haitian-Americans as an ethnic group, and government programs are beginning to be directed toward their community.

The importance of the school system to the integration of immigrants cannot be overestimated. Haitian students entering U.S. elementary and high schools face complex problems of adjustment. The language handicap is only one of their problems (Seligman 1977, Verdet 1976). So far the question of bilingual education for Creole-speaking immigrants has not been handled effectively. A detailed study of the plight of Haitian students in the New York school system could be a first step toward improving the situation.

Another area that is crucial for the survival of the population is the way in which its health problems are solved.[3] Haitian concepts of illness and cure are culture-specific. More detailed research is needed on the epidemiological characteristics of the Haitian-American population. Such a study would shed light on the ways Haitians cope with illness, and would also improve the delivery of health care in the Haitian-American community.

This analysis of the Haitian-American community adds a fundamental point to the refining of a theory of ethnicity: generational, class, and racial factors are as important as the ethnic factor to an understanding of the process of adaptation of minority groups in

3. It was not the goal of this research to study mental health problems among Haitian-Americans. According to Dr. Jean Alcé, a Haitian psychiatrist with the Kings County Psychiatric Center, "Haitian immigrants occupy more than 20 percent of the 300 beds for patients being treated for emotional disorders" (*New York Times*, June 26, 1979).

the United States. The decomposition of ethnicity as a sociological variable means the recognition of its behavioral, ideological, and symbolic content. This content is a reflection of the social class to which one belongs and may vary from one generation to the next. The group's perception of itself is shaped by the perceptions of the wider society. Thus the decoding of the symbolic systems of the national culture and the ethnic subculture provides a contextual framework for the interpretation of ethnicity.

Ethnic consciousness is not static; it is adaptable to external circumstances. The dependence situation of an ethnic group leaves its mark on the group's consciousness and consequently on the manifestation and manipulation of its ethnicity. In this sense, the Haitian-American community in New York presents us with a good case of dependent ethnicity because of its structural position in the total system.

Further research is needed for a better understanding of the integration of Haitian-Americans in the New York social landscape. It is my hope that others will join in this effort to help the Haitian-American community to understand its strengths and its weaknesses, and to recommend the best course of action for its survival and its integration in the mainstream of American society.

Appendix: Haitian Immigrants in the United States: A Historical Overview

The history of the Haitian immigrants in the United States has yet to be written. The historical records of the eighteenth and nineteenth centuries tend to be biased toward the contributions of some immigrants and silent about those of others. There have been three main waves of Haitian emigration to the United States. Refugees from the Haitian revolution of 1791–1803 included colonists, free mulattoes, and slaves. They settled primarily in New Orleans, New York, Boston, Norfolk, Philadelphia, and Charleston (Babb 1954, Hartridge 1943, A.N. Hunt 1975). During the United States' occupation of Haiti, from 1915 to 1934, a second wave of immigrants settled in New York, mainly in Harlem (Reid 1939). The largest group of Haitians began to migrate to the United States in 1957, when François Duvalier was elected president of the Republic of Haiti (Souffrant 1974, Fontaine 1976, Laguerre 1980a).

Afro–Saint-Dominguan and Haitian Immigrants, 1526–1914

As early as 1526 a few immigrants from Hispaniola were living in North America (Wood 1974:3). Later, when Louisiana was a French territory, there was a continuous population movement between Saint-Domingue and New Orleans. In 1747 Stephen La Rue, a free mulatto from Saint-Domingue, learned the folly of responding to insults by whites when he passed three white soldiers on a road near New Orleans. One of them called to him, "Bon soir, Seigneur Nigritte" (Good evening, Mr. Little Negro). The proud La Rue promptly replied, "Bon soir, Seigneur Jean Foutre" (Good evening, Mr. Fool). He was brutally beaten and taken to jail (Sterkx 1972:32). This little incident gives us a glimpse at the racial problems and insults to which the early immigrants were subjected.

A few years before the independence of America, Jean-Baptiste Point Du Sable, a mulatto born in Saint-Domingue about 1745 and educated in Paris, emigrated to Louisiana to develop a trading business along the Mississippi River. Business took him eventually to Peoria, Illinois, where he met an Indian woman named Kittahawa of the Potawatami tribe. They married and Du Sable settled there. In 1772 he built a trading hut at the mouth of the Chicago River, and two years later he moved his family there. They were the first permanent settlers at the site of what was to be the city of Chicago (Graham 1953:174; Spear 1967:5). The site of Du Sable's hut, now occupied by the Kirk soap factory, at the corner of Pine and Kinzie streets, is commemorated by a plaque on the factory wall. In Chicago today two public institutions, a high school and a museum, bear the name of this great trader and explorer from Saint-Domingue.

Afro–Saint-Dominguans made their first important contribution to this country at a critical moment in U.S. history. In 1779 a troop of 800 men of color from Saint-Domingue fought on behalf of American independence at the Battle of Savannah. They were disciplined and courageous men who believed in the freedom of nations to choose their own form of government (Schomburg 1921: 200, Laurent 1976). Their stiff resistance to the British troops was an important factor in the American victory.

As customarily happens among military men in a foreign land, some Afro–Saint-Dominguan soldiers fathered the offspring of American women. The history of these people of Saint-Dominguan descent is known more through oral traditions in Georgia than through history books.

The Saint-Dominguan army men learned much about military tactics and techniques during their stay in the United States. This combat experience helped some of them to strengthen their own ideas about the eventual independence of Haiti. Henri Christophe, who played a commanding role in the Haitian revolution and became king of Haiti (1807–20), had fought at Savannah. The tactics he learned there were probably used during the Haitian revolution (Quarles 1961:82, Logan 1941:25).

In the beginning of the Haitian rebellion, many colonists came to the United States to live until it was safe to return to the island. Some brought slaves with them.[1] Also arriving were *gens de couleur* who were ambivalent about the outcome of the revolution and the economic future of Saint-Domingue. These refugees constituted a large segment of the Saint-Dominguan population in the United States (Hartridge 1944).

One of the most distinguished among the Saint-Dominguan émigrés was Médéric-Louis-Elie Moreau de Saint-Méry. Born in Martinique and educated in Paris—he had a law degree—Moreau de Saint-Méry went to Saint-Domingue and worked there as a lawyer and an officeholder in the colonial administration. He was among the first émigrés to leave Saint-Domingue when the revolution started. He settled in Norfolk, where there was a concentration of Saint-Dominguan émigrés, probably in 1791, and remained there until 1793. The following year he established a bookstore and printing press in Philadelphia. He lived in Philadelphia until 1798 (Mims 1947:xvi).

Moreau de Saint-Méry's bookstore, at the corner of First and Walnut streets, shortly became the meetingplace of concerned émigrés eager to return to Saint-Domingue. *Le Courrier de la France et des Colonies,* a daily newspaper edited by Louis Gatereau and printed at Moreau de Saint-Méry's press from October 1795 to March 1796, was very popular among the émigrés because it carried news of recent developments on the island. Moreau de Saint-Méry wrote and published important books on Saint-Domingue: the two-volume *Description topographique et politique de la partie espagnole de l'isle de Saint-Domingue* (1796) and *Description topographique, physique, civile, politique, et historique de la partie française de l'isle de Saint-Domingue,* also in two volumes (1797). He was not the only émigré in Philadelphia

1. The news of the slave revolt in Saint-Domingue spread quickly among American planters and instilled fears that the newly arrived slaves from the island would incite American slaves to revolt (A. N. Hunt 1975, Babb 1954, Ottley and Weatherby 1967).

to write about Saint-Domingue; one Dalmas, another émigré, wrote the *Histoire de la révolution de Saint-Domingue*.

Life in Philadelphia was not easy for the Saint-Dominguan refugees. They had to start all over again, and some of them had at times to do the kind of work they previously had forced on their slaves. One Collot, son of a "former President of the High Council of Cap-François, and former officer in the Orleans Dragoons," made and sold ice cream (Moreau de Saint-Méry 1947:223).

Gens de couleur and slaves constituted a prominent segment of the Philadelphia émigré population. Free mulattoes formed their own exclusive group (Childs 1940:56). Some were very much involved in opposition politics. Political groupings of *gens de couleur* could be found in Baltimore, Norfolk, Charleston, and New Orleans as well as in Philadelphia (Woodson 1919:155).

The diary of Moreau de Saint-Méry testifies to the diversity of the Saint-Dominguan population in the United States:

> March 9, 1794. I met several colonists [in Portsmouth] whom I had known in Cap-François. . . . I couldn't help smiling scornfully when I heard one of them bewailing the fate that had reduced him to only two Negro servants.
>
> April 3. We met Dénard from Cap-François. He dined with us the following day.
>
> April 4. My mother-in-law and Gauvain arrived from Baltimore after a three-day voyage. With my mother-in-law was her little Héloise, born at Cap-François May 22, 1785, and her griffon, Sylvie.
>
> So many were congregated in our house [in Norfolk] that we were obliged to employ a cook—a young Negress named Louise belonging to M. Crousielles, a refugee from Saint-Domingue, living in Portsmouth.
>
> May 14. Mme Bayard, born Mlle Fage, died. She was the wife of the former assessor-counselor to the Council of Cap-François.
>
> July 25. I went to a concert at the house of Désèze, son of the counselor of Cap-François. This interesting young man ran a pension in New York.

Sept. 12. I saw Dr. Valentin of Norfolk in New York. He had been a physician at Cap-François. [Moreau de Saint-Méry 1947:42–45, 125, 128, 143]

Another prominent Saint-Dominguan émigré was the naturalist John James Audubon. Born in Cayes, Saint-Domingue, on April 26, 1785, he emigrated to the United States during the summer of 1803. In 1812 he was naturalized an American citizen. Audubon has left his name in American natural history. His drawings of birds in America are still an invaluable source of information for naturalists and ornithologists (Ford 1964:424–25).

Emigré colonists brought many slaves with them to the United States. "The infamous Caradeux," for example, "fled to the United States with sixty slaves" (Mackenzie 1830:34). Roland Wingfield (1966:35–40) estimates that "the exodus of French colonists, which began in 1791 and climaxed in 1802, brought about 10,000 planters, *gens de couleur* and their respective slaves to New Orleans." The development of voodoo in New Orleans as an organized cult was probably due to the emigration of Saint-Dominguan slaves to Louisiana. To combat voodooism, the Municipal Council of New Orleans issued in 1817 an ordinance whereby slaves were permitted to congregate for dancing purposes only on Sundays, and only in Congo Square (Tallant 1971:28).

Marie Laveau, known as the "voodoo queen of New Orleans," was born of émigré Haitian parents. She married a carpenter from Haiti at St. Louis Cathedral in New Orleans in 1819. When her husband died, she married Captain Christophe Glapion, a Haitian migrant who was prominent in New Orleans and had "served with distinction in the battalion of men of Santo Domingo, under D'Aquin, with [Andrew] Jackson in the war of 1815" (Tallant 1971:62). Jackson rewarded the leader of that battalion, Joseph Savary, for distinguished service by appointing him second major—the first black to hold this position in the U.S. Army (McConnell 1968:71).

Two other Haitian-Americans also left their mark on Louisiana history. Victor Séjour, the mulatto son of a Saint-Domingue émigré to New Orleans, wrote "many plays that were presented on the stage in Paris and became one of the secretaries of Napoleon III" (Logan 1941:48); and Julien Déjour, born in Haiti in

1850 and reared by a Louisiana family, became known for his works of charity in New Orleans (Desdunes 1973:94).

Haitian immigrants have left their mark as well on the architecture of Louisiana and South Carolina. "Many of the buildings of Old Charleston were constructed according to plans of the émigrés from Saint Domingue and . . . the justly famous wrought iron railings of many of the buildings in the Vieux Carré of New Orleans were forged by slaves from there" (Logan 1941: 47–48). Emigrés built the kind of houses to which they were accustomed in Saint-Domingue—shotgun houses, which were "small, usually rectangular buildings, one room wide (no more than 12 feet across); three rooms deep, all connected to each other; and with doors at each end" (Vlach 1977:51; see also Vlach 1975).

> The size of the [New Orleans black] community was greatly increased in 1809 by the immigration of approximately 2,100 Haitian mulattoes, who first emigrated to Cuba but were later forced off the island by anti-French sentiment. At the same time, a like number of slaves arrived from Haiti, including many who were relatives of free blacks. By 1810, blacks outnumbered whites in New Orleans, 10,500 to 4,500. Such a population expansion necessitated new housing. As many carpenters, masons and inhabitants were Haitian, it was only natural that they modeled their new homes on those they had left behind. [Vlach 1977:52]

Many Saint-Dominguan refugees settled with their slaves in what was to be known as St. Mary's Parish in Charleston. The parish records of St. Mary's Church, now a historical landmark, attest to the diversity of regional origins of these émigrés. Natives of Cailles, Môle Saint-Nicolas, Jacmel, and Cap François had crowded together on passenger ships bound for South Carolina.

Afro–Saint-Dominguan émigrés in New York City could easily be distinguished from other New Yorkers by their manner of dress: "Creoles from Haiti flounced through the streets clad richly in West Indian materials; 'coal black negresses,' in flowing white dresses and colorful turbans made of mouchoir de madras, strolled with white or mixed creoles, adding to the picturesqueness of the scene" (Ottley and Weatherby 1967:47).

Among the slaves brought to New York by the Saint-Dominguan émigrés, one man in particular stands out. Pierre Toussaint is still venerated in Catholic circles in New York for his works of charity. He was born in 1766 on the plantation of a Frenchman named Bérard, in the parish of St. Marc, Saint-Domingue. All of the Toussaint family belonged to the Bérards. When Bérard emigrated to New York in 1787, "he took with him five servants, including Toussaint and his sister Rosalie" (Lee 1854:2). Eventually Bérard returned to Haiti, but before he left New York he paid one Pierre Merchant $50 to teach Pierre Toussaint the art of hairdressing. With his earnings as a hairdresser Toussaint managed to buy his own and his sister's freedom. His clientele included some of the wealthiest people in the city. After his marriage in 1811 to Claudine Gaston, a Haitian nurse, Toussaint bought a home on Franklin Street. The city directory of 1845 provides the following information: "Peter Toussaint, home 144 Franklin Street. Shop 141 Canal Street" (Sheehan and Sheehan 1955:218).

After Bérard died in Haiti, Toussaint became the economic supporter of his widow. Despite the social distance that separated them, a deep friendship grew between Toussaint and Mme Bérard. His generosity was felt also by Catholic charities, institutions, and seminarians. When he died in 1853, the Irish priest who delivered the eulogy at his funeral mass assured the mourners that "there are few left among the clergy superior to him in devotion and zeal for the Church and for the glory of God; among laymen, none" (Sheehan and Sheehan 1955:230). Pierre Toussaint was a deeply religious man.[2]

The history of Haitian settlement in the United States in the middle and late nineteenth century is not well known.[3] A few

2. In 1951 Francis Cardinal Spellman submitted Pierre Toussaint's name to the Vatican for consideration for canonization. Since then, a continuing effort has been aimed at making his life known among church members and the people of New York.

3. Shortly after the independence of Haiti in 1804, Dessalines encouraged émigré blacks and mulattoes to return from America, and offered $40 to American ship captains for each such man they brought back to Haiti (Basket 1818:296).

Since the early nineteenth century, some American blacks have sought a country where blacks could settle. From about 1824 to 1864, various attempts were made to settle in Haiti (Hunt 1860, Wesley 1919). In 1824, with the help of a Haitian agent, 13,000 black Americans settled there (Montague 1956:74–75, Logan 1941:308–10). During the administration of Faustin-Elie Soulouque (1847–58), people achieved some kind of upward mobility. Charles L. Reason, whose parents were Haitian, was "Professor of BellesLettres and of the French Language and Adjutant-Professor of Mathematics in the New York Central College, McGraville, Cortlandt County, N.Y.," about 1849 (Simmons 1968:1105). William De Florville, known as Billy the Barber, was the personal barber and confidant of Abraham Lincoln. According to an editorial in the *Illinois State Journal*, "only two men in Springfield understood Lincoln, his law partner, William H. Herndon, and his barber, William De Florville" (Washington 1942:190). It is likely that Lincoln's policy toward black Americans and the Republic of Haiti was influenced by such black friends as Billy the Barber.[4]

Haitian Immigrants, 1915–56

In the first half of the twentieth century one of the country's outstanding pharmaceutical schools was the Patrick School of Pharmacy in Boston. Its founder, Dr. Thomas W. Patrick, had been born in Haiti in 1872 and educated in Trinidad; most of his students were white. An alumnus of his school was the first person to be granted a pharmacist's license by the Massachusetts Board of Registration. Dr. Patrick was known internationally and his school trained a good number of American pharmacists.

The succession of provisional presidents that swept Haiti from 1900 to 1915 led to the United States' occupation of the island republic and to an increase in the emigration of Haitians to the United States. From 1920 on, Harlem experienced a turmoil of political activities with the Harlem Renaissance and Marcus Garvey's Back-to-Africa movement. Haitian émigrés participated in the cultural and political activities of both movements.

Emile Desdunes was stationed in New Orleans "to arrange the expatriation of all Creoles of color who wished to leave the city" (Desdunes 1973:112; see also Bell 1959:132–42). In 1861 James Redpart, an abolitionist militant, was charged with helping blacks to emigrate to Haiti. That year 12,000 black Americans made the journey (Souffrant 1974:137, Holly and Harris 1970). Among the first such migrants was the grandfather of W. E. B. Du Bois, who went to Haiti in 1821 but returned to the United States in 1830 (Du Bois 1968:68).

4. The United States recognized Haiti's independence during Lincoln's administration. Lincoln also attempted to resettle freed American slaves in Haiti.

Haitian immigrants did not form a ghetto within Harlem's black community; they were dispersed throughout the district. Males outnumbered females in the Haitian population (Reid 1939:81). Most Haitian immigrants were political exiles and traders. They tended to be better educated than the majority of Harlem blacks, and in general were more leftist than their American neighbors (Reid 1939:96).

The New York Haitians tried to interest the black population in Haitian goods. The function of such organizations as Utilités d'Haïti was to import and promote honey, coffee, and rum from Haiti. Aside from the economic gain, they were concerned to help the economy of the island under the U.S. occupation.

These Haitians had migrated legally from Haiti's cities. Their education and sophistication fitted them for a diversity of white-collar jobs. Ira Reid (1939:97) found that they were "usually engaged in industry, trade or the professions. Few, if any, of these persons [were] found in domestic service." During this period Haitians started to send their children to American universities. Teachers College of Columbia University provided a few scholarships to the Haitian government for that purpose. Few of these children had received Catholic educations. Reid (1939:97) points out that "Catholicism, the State religion in Haiti, loses effectiveness in the United States as the Haitians' children are refused admission to certain parochial schools."

Some Haitians occupied key positions in the Universal Negro Improvement Association (UNIA), Marcus Garvey's movement. Among the many Haitian officials was Jean-Joseph Adam, who was the official translator for the UNIA mission to the League of Nations. He became later UNIA ambassador to France (Vincent 1972:110). Eliézer Cadet, a Haitian diplomat who represented the UNIA at the Pan-African Congress in Paris in 1919, played a strategic role in the movement (Contee 1970, Martin 1976:122). When Haitian Garveyites Napoléon Francis, Eli Garcia, and Théodore Stephens were expelled from the island, they settled in New York. Eli Garcia was to become a UNIA diplomat and auditor and an official of the Black Star Line (Vincent 1972:121). Other Haitians shunned the Back-to-Africa movement in favor of the Communist party. Jacques Roumain became one of the most outspoken Communists of the early 1930s.

At the end of the U.S. occupation of Haiti in 1934, some American marines who had Haitian mistresses, wives, and children made special efforts to bring them to the United States. Since then, every coup d'état in Haiti has brought a handful of refugees to American soil. After World War II, Haitian women were drawn to New York, Washington, Chicago, Evanston, and Los Angeles to work as sleep-in maids in white American homes (Woldemikael 1980). A few Haitian professionals also came in search of work. Most such people had made earlier contacts with Americans in Haiti who were able to find work for them in the United States. At that time it was less difficult to get a resident visa. Most of these people, however, had no intention of staying; their aim was to make enough money to enable them to live comfortably in Haiti. They therefore made no effort to bring their families with them. In New York they were dispersed throughout the city. As an immigrant who arrived there in the early 1950s pointed out: "Scattered through the city, very often, they had to travel long distances to meet one of their compatriots. . . . One place where you could find many of them was the mess-hall of Horn and Hardart Cafeterias" (*Unité*, September 30, 1976). When President Magloire received an honorary degree from Fordham University in 1955, there were ample numbers of Haitians in the city to welcome him and make their presence felt.

Haitian Immigrants, 1957–80

After Magloire was forced out of office in 1956, he and some of his associates settled in Queens. Such defeated presidential candidates as Louis Déjoie and Daniel Fignolé also came as refugees, as did their close collaborators. Several members of the opposition, however, remained in Port-au-Prince, hoping to change the course of events by continued involvement in politics under the Duvalier administration. The invasion attempts in 1959 and in the early 1960s brought reprisals against Duvalier's opponents, and large numbers of politicians, students, and professionals left the country. Other politicians who were not in jail left shortly after Papa Doc was elected president for life in 1964. Until 1971, Haitian emigration was made up primarily of the elite and the educated middle class. From 1972 on, however, the urban proletariat, peasants, and Haitians who previously worked in the Bahamas have been reaching the United States in leaky wooden sailboats (see also D. Marshall 1979).

From 1959 to 1977, 76,982 Haitian immigrants were admitted to the United States (Laguerre 1983:134). The great majority came directly from Haiti or had lived previously in the United States. From 1969 to 1977, 2,529 Haitians were granted the status of resident aliens because their spouses were U.S. citizens. More Haitian men (1,701, or 67.26 percent) were able to become permanent residents through marriage to Americans than Haitian women (828, or 32.74 percent). The majority of U.S. citizens involved in such marriages appear also to be of Haitian origin.

From 1962 to 1977, more Haitian females (39,640, or 52.21 percent) were admitted as resident aliens than Haitian males (34,853, or 46.79 percent). The majority of males admitted were in the age bracket 10–39 (Laguerre 1983:135). In 1977, a representative year, 627 (24.71 percent) were in the age bracket 10–19, 597 (23.53 percent) were in the age bracket 20–29, and 651 (25.66 percent) were in the age bracket 30–39. Among the Haitian females admitted during the same year, 650 (22.38 percent) were in the age bracket 10–19, 652 (22.45 percent) were in the age bracket 20–29, and 592 (20.39 percent) were in the age bracket 30–39. In 1977, 73.90 percent of all Haitian males and 65.22 percent of all Haitian females admitted were in the age group 10–39; 7.96 percent of the females admitted were under 9 years of age, in comparison with 9.70 percent of males. The male population, then, is slightly younger than the female population.

Table 6 provides a profile of the occupational structure of legal Haitian immigrants during 1966–77. Here again 1977 will serve as a reference point. During that year 14 percent of those in the work force held white-collar jobs as professionals, managers, and administrators. An additional 14.2 percent were engaged in clerical work. Those immigrants who had engaged in farm labor in Haiti did not necessarily do so here. Only 1.4 percent were either farmers or farm workers, while 51.7 percent worked as operatives, laborers, and service workers.

From 1962 to 1977, 12,575 Haitian immigrants became naturalized U.S. citizens (Table 7): 46.4 percent males and 53.6 percent

Table 6. Occupations of legal Haitian immigrants in U.S. work force, 1966–77

Year	Number admitted	Immigrants not in work force		Total number in work force	Professional and technical workers		Managers and administrators		Sales workers		Clerical workers		Craft workers	
		Number	Percent		Number	Percent	Number	Percent	Number	Percent	Number	Percent	Number	Percent
1977	5,441	2,889	53.1%	2,552	270	10.5%	90	3.5%	14	0.5%	363	14.2%	242	9.4%
1976	5,410	3,313	61.2	2,097	234	11.1	84	4.0	17	0.8	256	12.2	262	12.4
1975	5,145	2,920	56.8	2,225	232	10.4	120	5.4	26	1.2	204	9.2	432	19.4
1974	3,946	2,286	57.9	1,660	167	10.1	63	3.8	6	0.4	161	9.7	283	17.0
1973	4,786	3,291	68.8	1,495	223	14.9	69	4.6	13	0.9	144	9.6	219	14.6
1972	5,809	4,066	70.0	1,743	394	22.6	73	4.2	13	0.7	162	9.3	216	12.4
1971	7,444	4,973	66.8	2,471	592	24.0	60	2.4	19	0.8	196	7.9	601	24.3
1970	6,932	2,682	38.7	4,250	694	16.3	49	1.2	22	0.5	417	9.8	1,418	33.4
1969	6,542	3,151	48.2	3,391	663	19.6	65	1.9	19	0.6	284	8.4	960	28.3
1968	6,806	3,702	54.4	3,104	669	21.6	96	3.1	12	0.4	222	7.2	574	18.5
1967	3,567	1,996	56.0	1,571	307	19.5	60	3.8	9	0.6	121	7.7	163	10.4
1966	3,801	2,118	55.7	1,683	353	21.0	106	6.3	23	1.4	221	13.1	250	14.9

Year	Operatives		Transport equipment workers		Laborers		Farmers		Farm workers		Service workers		Domestics (private household)	
	Number	Percent	Number	Percent	Number	Percent	Number	Percent	Number	Percent	Number	Percent	Number	Percent
1977	829	32.4%	103	4.0%	67	2.6%	3	0.1%	35	1.3%	326	12.7%	210	8.2%
1976	709	33.8	69	3.2	60	2.8	10	0.4	34	1.6	224	10.6	138	6.3
1975	738	33.2	54	2.4	68	3.1	2	0.1	27	1.2	199	8.9	123	5.5
1974	568	34.2	35	2.1	71	4.3	1	0.1	26	1.6	192	11.6	87	5.2
1973	532	35.6	–	–	19	1.3	–	–	10	0.7	152	10.2	114	7.6
1972	525	30.0	–	–	12	0.7	–	–	19	1.1	159	9.1	170	9.8
1971	707	28.6	–	–	20	0.8	7	0.3	14	0.6	154	6.2	101	4.1
1970	1,230	28.9	–	–	9	0.2	21	0.5	2	–	169	4.0	219	5.2
1969	718	21.2	–	–	17	0.5	9	0.3	6	0.2	178	5.2	472	13.9
1968	715	23.0	–	–	16	0.5	1	–	10	0.3	144	4.6	645	20.8
1967	400	25.5	–	–	10	0.6	–	–	2	0.1	76	4.8	423	26.9
1966	447	26.6	–	–	21	1.2	5	0.3	12	0.7	94	5.6	151	9.0

SOURCE: *Immigration and Naturalization Service Annual Reports*, 1966–77.

females. Haitian immigrants have been slow to become U.S. citizens, but the numbers of those who have done so have grown considerably since 1971, when Jean-Claude Duvalier became president for life. Many have acquired citizenship in order to be able to sponsor their relatives and to have some protection when they return to Haiti for visits. During 1977, 82.56 percent of male Haitians who were naturalized U.S. citizens were in the age bracket 20–49 years, in comparison with 83.57 percent of the female population. Young men and women under 20 years of age represent respectively 4.39 and 5.48 percent of the naturalized male and female immigrants. Of the naturalized men, 13.05 percent were 50 years old or more, in comparison with 10.96 percent of the naturalized women.

The Haitian population is distributed unevenly in almost all of the states, possessions, and territories of the United States. No Haitian immigrant, however, was reported living in Alaska, South Dakota, or Guam (Laguerre 1983a:143). New York is by far the preferred site of resettlement. It is estimated that from 1956 to 1977, 76.40 percent (47,118) of the total Haitian immigrant population lived there. The second major area of settlement is Florida,

Table 7. Haitians naturalized as U.S. citizens, by sex, 1962–77

	Males		Females		
Year	Number	Percent	Number	Percent	Total
1977	866	46.31%	1,004	53.69%	1,870
1976	1,190	44.74	1,470	55.26	2,660
1975	913	46.64	1,053	53.36	1,966
1974	683	45.96	803	54.04	1,486
1973	453	44.63	562	55.37	1,015
1972	392	48.28	420	51.72	812
1971	295	53.25	259	46.75	554
1970	226	52.19	207	47.81	433
1969	145	51.42	137	48.58	282
1968	126	41.58	177	58.42	303
1967	116	47.35	129	52.65	245
1966	103	43.28	135	56.72	238
1965	94	43.32	123	56.68	217
1964	80	48.78	84	51.22	164
1963	94	47.24	105	52.76	199
1962	59	45.04	72	54.96	131

SOURCE: *Immigration and Naturalization Service Annual Reports*, 1962–77.

with 2,791 Haitians (4.53 percent). Massachusetts holds 4.44 percent (2,740), New Jersey 4.29 percent (2,644), and Illinois 4.20 percent (2,590). Nearly 80 percent of the population lived in large cities: New York (69.19 percent), Miami (3.86 percent), Chicago (3.39 percent), Boston (1.12 percent), Washington, D.C. (0.85 percent), and Newark (0.76 percent).

Until 1972, most undocumented Haitian immigrants had arrived as tourists and overstayed their visas. Since that year, however, large numbers of Haitian boat people have arrived in Florida. Most of these people are former residents of the Bahamas and desperate peasants who felt that under Jean-Claude Duvalier they had no chance for economic improvement and political security.

The first boatload of Haitians arrived at West Palm Beach from the Bahamas on September 15, 1963 (U.S. Congress, Senate, 1975). All twenty-five passengers claimed political asylum; it was denied. Sailboats did not become a general means of migration, however, until 1972. On December 13 of that year 65 Haitians—42 men, 20 women, 3 children—reached Florida after "a three-week journey aboard a leaking 56-foot sailboat" (*New York Times*, December 13, 1972). More were to follow: 25 on April 17, 1973; 12 on May 22; 6 during the first week of June; 62 on September 24 (*Haiti-Observateur*, December 15–22, 1972; April 20–27, July 20–27, October 5–12, 1973; *Miami Star-Ledger*, May 23, 1973). Three years later, during the last week of September 1976, 132 Haitian refugees arrived in Miami (*Patriote Haïtien*, September 10–30, 1976); 179 arrived during the week of August 14–21, 1977 (*En Avant*, September 1977). More than 10,000 came here during the spring of 1980. While on the high seas, such refugees survived mainly "by drinking sea water and eating raw fish" (U.S. Congress, Senate, 1975:36). According to Judge James Lawrence King (1980:1), "perhaps thirty thousand Haitians have flocked to the shores of South Florida over the past twenty years, fleeing the most repressive government in the Americas."

The refugees left Haiti in search of political security in a country where they would no longer be subjected to harassment by the Tontons Macoutes and where they could live peacefully without fear of being sent to the infamous Fort Dimanche jail. Upon their arrival in the United States, they were jailed. The Reverend Jack Cassidy, minister of the United Church of Christ, has

> visited in the jails, particularly the jail in Immokelee [Florida] prior [to] and during the hunger strike. Here we have 82 men in the county stockade. There are two cells, 41 men in each cell, 35 by 45. By the admission of the attendants at the Immokelee jail, the stockade was so understaffed that they could not even provide a daily opportunity for these men to get outside of the cell except to eat in a small adjoining room. [U.S. Congress, Senate, 1975:12]

Mistreatment of Haitian political refugees has been protested by other ethnic leaders and humanitarian groups. On February 14, 1974, a picket line outside the Federal Building in San Francisco was organized by the Berkeley and San Francisco chapters of the U.S. Committee for Justice to Latin American Political Prisoners. Another picket line outside the State Department offices in Washington was organized by about 200 people in support of the granting of asylum to Haitian refugees (*Militant*, March 1, 1974). Howard M. Squadron, chairman of the National Governing Council of the American Jewish Congress, in a letter to Assistant Secretary of State Francis L. Kellogg, in charge of refugee and migration affairs, called on the State Department to grant political asylum to the Haitian refugees. He charged the State Department with "racial bias" in its handling of the Haitian situation and pointed out that white Cubans were "liberally admitted into the U.S. under virtually identical circumstances" (American Jewish Congress *News*, July 22, 1974). Infuriated about the inhuman way in which the Haitian refugees were treated in Miami, Archbishop Coleman F. Carroll declared, "I have a dog that gets better treatment than these people" (*Miami Herald*, July 3, 1974). During a Senate hearing Ira Gollobin, an attorney in New York City, put it this way: "I challenge anyone to find any other category of persons facing the issue of life and death who are treated in such a manner as to deprive them of elementary due process rights, as well as the rights that are accorded them under the Protocol Relating to the Status of Refugees" (U.S. Congress, Senate, 1975).[5]

5. On the legal issues involved in the Haitian refugees' applications for political asylum, see J. L. King 1980, Schey 1981, Wampler 1980. A brief summary of some of these legal issues can be found in Gollobin 1979. For journalistic treatments see Wortham 1980 and Bogre 1979. Two major congressional hearings were held on the question of Haitian immigration. The proceedings of these hearings contain a wealth of witnesses' accounts and depositions by individuals and organizations that support the granting of political asylum to the Haitian refugees (U.S. Congress, House, 1976, 1980). See also Ryan 1982, Bruck 1982.

In a 179-page Final Order Granting Relief, Judge James Lawrence King found (1980) that the U.S. Immigration and Naturalization Service had used discriminatory practices to prevent Haitian refugees from being seriously considered for refugee status:

> One central issue . . . overshadows this entire case: unlawful discrimination. The plaintiffs charge that they faced a transparently discriminatory program designed to deport Haitian nationals and no one else. The uncontroverted evidence proves their claim. [P. 2]
>
> The plaintiffs are part of the first substantial flights of black refugees from a repressive regime to this country. All of the plaintiffs are black. In contrast, for example, only a relatively small percent of the Cuban refugees who have fled to this country are black. Prior to the most recent Cuban exodus, all of the Cubans who sought political asylum in individual 8 C.F.R. Sec. 108 hearings were granted asylum routinely. None of the over 4,000 Haitians processed during the INS "Program" at issue in this lawsuit were granted asylum. No greater disparity can be imagined. [P. 3]
>
> Immigration judges were a functioning part of the Haitian program. Having received orders from the Chief Immigration Judge, they tripled the number of hearings, forced Haitians to plead to alienage, and joined with the District Director in setting unreasonable time limits for filing asylum applications. As a result, Haitians were deprived of rights normally available to aliens in deportation proceedings, and the opportunity to adequately prepare their asylum applications. The judges contributed to an accelerated program the purpose and effect of which was to deny Haitians asylum. [P. 145]
>
> Those Haitians who came to the U.S. seeking freedom and justice did not find it. Instead, they were confronted with an Immigration and Naturalization Service determined to deport them. The decision was made among high INS officials to expel Haitians, despite whatever claims to asylum individual Haitians might have. A program was set up to accomplish this goal. The program resulted in wholesale violations of due process, and only Haitians were affected. [P. 162]
>
> In reaching its conclusions the Court has listened to a wealth of in-Court testimony, examined numerous depositions, and read hundreds of documents submitted by the parties. Much of the evidence is both shocking and brutal, populated by the ghosts of individual

Haitians—including those who have been returned from the U.S.—who have been beaten, tortured and left to die in Haitian prisons. Much of the evidence is not brutal but simply callous—evidence that INS officials decided to ship all Haitians back to Haiti simply because their continued presence in the United States had become a problem. The manner in which INS treated the more than 4,000 Haitian plaintiffs violated the Constitution, the immigration statutes, international agreements, INS regulations and INS operating procedures. It must stop. [P. 4]

References Cited

Acosta, Mercedes. 1973. Azúcar e inmigración haitiana. In *Azúcar y política en la República Dominicana*, ed. André Corten et al., pp. 115–54. Santo Domingo: Ediciones de Taller.

Ade, E. 1978. Notes sur la population et l'économie d'Haïti: Importance de la malnutrition et des problèmes sanitaires en cet endroit. *Cahiers de Nutrition et de Diététique* 13:21–26.

Adriyin, Antouan. 1973. Problèm lévé ti ayisyin nouyok (Problems in the socialization of Haitian children in New York). *Sel* 10:31–37.

Anderson, Grace M. 1974. *Networks of Contact: The Portuguese of Toronto*. Waterloo: Wilfrid Laurier University Publications.

Anderson, Jervis. 1975. The Haitians of New York. *New Yorker*, March 31, pp. 50–55.

Ardener, Shirley. 1964. The Comparative Study of Rotating Credit Associations. *Journal of the Royal Anthropological Institute* 44:201–29.

Babb, Winston Chandler. 1954. French Refugees from Saint-Domingue to the Southern United States, 1791–1810. Ph.D. dissertation, University of Virginia.

Bajeux, Jean Claude. 1973. Les Haïtiens en République Dominicaine: Mirage et réalités. *Sel* 10:13–20.

Bales, Robert F. 1950. *Interaction Process Analysis*. Cambridge, Mass.: Addison-Wesley.

Barth, Fredrik. 1969. *Ethnic Groups and Boundaries*. Boston: Little, Brown.

Bascom, William R. 1952. The Esusu. *Journal of the Royal Anthropological Institute* 82(1):63–69.

Basket, Sir James. 1818. *History of the Island of St. Domingo, from Its Discovery to the Present Period*. London.

Bastide, Roger, Françoise Morin, and François Raveau. 1974. *Les Haïtiens en France*. Paris: Mouton.

Bastien, Rémy. 1951. *La familia rural haitiana*. Mexico City: Libra.

1961. Haitian Rural Family Organization. *Social and Economic Studies* 10(4):478–510.

Becker, Marshall H., et al. 1975. Sociobehavioral Determinants of Compliance with Health and Medical Care Recommendations. *Medical Care* 13:10–24.

Béghin, Ivan, et al. 1965a. Le Centre de Récupération pour Enfants Malnourris du Fond-Parisien (Haiti): Rapport préliminaire sur le fonctionnement du Centre et résultat des quatre premiers mois d'activité. *Annales de la Société Belge de Médecine Tropicale* 45:557–76.

1965b. Enquête clinique sur l'état de nutrition des enfants préscolaires du Fond-Parisien et de Ganthier (Haiti), Juin 1964. *Annales de la Société Belge de Médecine Tropicale* 45:577–602.

1970. *L'Alimentation et la nutrition en Haiti*. Paris: Presses Universitaires de France.

Bell, Howard H. 1959. The Negro Emigration Movement, 1849–1854: A Phase of Negro Nationalism. *Phylon* 20 (Summer):132–42.

Bernard, William S. 1975. *The United States and the Migration Process*. New York: American Immigration and Citizenship Conference.

Bernardin-Haldeman, Verena. 1972. Femmes haïtiennes à Montréal. Master's thesis, Université Laval, Quebec.

Blauner, Robert. 1972. *Racial Oppression in America*. New York: Harper & Row.

Bloch, Harriet. 1976. Changing Domestic Roles among Polish Immigrant Women. *Anthropological Quarterly* 49(1):3–10.

Blumer, Herbert. 1969. *Symbolic Interactionism*. Englewood Cliffs, N.J.: Prentice-Hall.

Bodson, Etienne, Pol Ripet, and Pierre Lefèvre. 1970. Haiti—70. Connaissance d'un pays. *Conflits* 28:1–68.

Bogre, Michelle. 1979. Haitian Refugees. *Migration Today* 7(4):9–11.

Boissevain, Jeremy. 1974. *Friends of Friends*. Oxford: Blackwell.

Bonnett, Aubrey W. 1980. An Examination of Rotating Credit Associations among Black West Indian Immigrants in Brooklyn. In *Sourcebook on the New Immigration: Implications for the United States and the International Community*, ed. Roy Bryce-Laporte, pp. 271–83. New Brunswick: Transaction Books.

Bott, Elizabeth. 1971. *Family and Social Network*. New York: Free Press.

Boulos, Carlos. 1954. Une Enquête alimentaire en Haiti. *Bulletin de l'Association Médicale Haïtienne* 6:3.

1955. Alimentation et grossesse. Réunions obstétricales mensuelles de la Maternité Isaie Jeanty. Port-au-Prince: Théodore.

Bourguignon, Erika. 1954. Dreams and Dream Interpretation in Haiti. *American Anthropologist* 56:262–68.

Bowering, J., R. L. Lowenberg, and M. A. Morrison. 1980. Nutritional studies of pregnant women in East Harlem, New York, USA. *American Journal of Clinical Nutrition* 33:1987–96.

Bruck, Connie. 1982. Springing the Haitians. *American Lawyer* 4 (September):35–40.

Bryce-Laporte, Roy S. 1972. Black Immigrants: The Experience of Invisibility and Inequality. *Journal of Black Studies* 1(3):29–56.

1979. New York City and the New Caribbean Immigration: A Contextual Statement. *International Migration Review* 13(2):214–34.

Buchanan, Susan H. 1979a. Haitian Women in New York City. *Migration Today* 7(4):19–25.

1979b. Language and Identity: Haitians in New York City. *International Migration Review* 13(2):298–313.

1980. Scattered Seeds: The Meaning of the Migration for Haitians in New York City. Ph.D. dissertation, New York University.

Bullough, Bonnie, and Vera L. Bullough. 1972. *Poverty, Ethnic Identity, and Health Care*. New York: Appleton-Century-Crofts.

Cando, Hansy, and Félix Jorge. 1966. Rupture révolutionnaire en Haïti. *Frères du Monde* 43–44:72–88.

Carlson, Guster G. 1939. Number Gambling: A Study of a Culture Complex. Ph.D. dissertation, University of Michigan.

Cassidy, Hugh J. B., and Edward Wakin. 1978. Saturday Night Voodoo: Sunday Morning Mass. *U.S. Catholic* 43(7):35–38.

Castor, Suzy. 1971. *La ocupación norteamericana de Haiti y sus consecuencias (1915–1934)*. Mexico City: Siglo Veintiuno.

Centers for Disease Control. 1982a. Gynecomastia in Haitians: Puerto Rico, Texas, New York. *MMWR [Morbidity and Mortality Weekly Report]*, April 30, pp. 205–6.

1982b. Follow-up of Gynecomastia among Haitian Males. *MMWR*, July 16, pp. 370–75.

1982c. Update on Kaposi's Sarcoma and Opportunistic Infections in Previously Healthy Persons: United States. *MMWR*, June 11, pp. 294–301.

1982d. A Cluster of Kaposi's Sarcoma and Pneumocystis Carinii Pneumonia among Homosexual Male Residents of Los Angeles and Orange Counties, California. *MMWR*, June 18, pp. 305–7.

César, Carmontel. 1955. *La Nutrition chez les femmes enceintes*. Réunions obstétricales mensuelles de la Maternité Isaie Jeanty. Port-au-Prince: Théodore.

Charles, Claude. 1979. Brief Comments on the Occurrence, Etiology, and Treatment of Indisposition. *Social Science and Medicine* 13B(2):135–36.

Childs, Frances Sergeant. 1940. *French Refugee Life in the United States, 1790–1800: An American Chapter of the French Revolution*. Baltimore: Johns Hopkins University Press.

Clark, G. F. 1921. First Report of Pelagra in Haiti. *U.S. Naval Medical Bulletin* 15:813–14.

Clark, Margaret. 1959. *Health in the Mexican-American Culture*. Berkeley: University of California Press.

Clérismé, Rénald. 1975. Dependency and Haitian Migration. A Case Study: Bassin-Bleuans in Brooklyn. Master's thesis, New York University.

Cohen, Abner. 1979. Political Symbolism. *Annual Review of Anthropology* 8:87–113.

Cohen, Abner, ed. 1974. *Urban Ethnicity*. London: Tavistock.

Cohen, Ronald. 1978. Ethnicity: Problem and Focus in Anthropology. *Annual Review of Anthropology* 7:379–403.

Comhaire, Suzanne, and Jean Comhaire. 1952. La alimentación en la región de Kenscoff, Haiti. *América Indígena* 12:177–203.

Connolly, Harold X. 1977. *A Ghetto Grows in Brooklyn*. New York: New York University Press.

Contee, C. G. 1970. The Worley Report on the Pan-African Congress of 1919. *Journal of Negro History* 55 (April):141.

Conway, Frederic James. 1978. Pentecostalism in the Context of Haitian Religion and Health Practice. Ph.D. dissertation, American University.

Crowley, Daniel J. 1953. American Credit Institutions of Yoruba Type. *Man* 53 (May):80.

Cruse, Harold. 1967. *The Crisis of the Negro Intellectual*. New York: Morrow.

Dahya, Badr. 1974. The Nature of Pakistani Ethnicity in Industrial Cities in Britain. In *Urban Ethnicity*, ed. Abner Cohen, pp. 77–118. London: Tavistock.

Dambreville, Charles. 1949. L'Alimentation des travailleurs. In *Premier Congrès National du Travail*. Port-au-Prince.

Daniel, Christophe-Jocelyn. 1977. *La Médecine traditionnelle en Haïti*. Ph.D. dissertation, Université de Bordeaux.

Davison, Robert B. 1962. *West Indian Migrants*. London: Oxford University Press.

Déjean, Paul. 1978. *Les Haitiens au Québec*. Montreal: Presses de l'Université du Québec.

Déjean, Yves. 1977. Le Bilinguisme et les enfants haïtiens. *Perspectives in Bilingual-Bicultural Education* 1:20–24.

Delbeau, Jean-Claude. 1969. La Médecine populaire en Haïti. Ph.D. dissertation, Université de Bordeaux.

Denis, Lorimer. 1963. Médecine populaire. *Bulletin du Bureau d'Ethnologie* (Port-au-Prince) 4:37–39.

Desdunes, Rodolphe Lucien. 1973. *Our People and Our History*. Baton Rouge: Louisiana State University Press.

Despres, Leo A. 1967. *Cultural Pluralism and Nationalist Politics in British Guiana*. Chicago: Rand McNally.

Despres, Leo A., ed. 1975. *Ethnicity and Resource Competition in Plural Societies*. The Hague: Mouton.

De Vos, George. 1980. Identity Problems of Immigrant Minorities: A Psychocultural Comparative Approach Applied to Korean Japanese. In *Sourcebook on the New Immigration,* ed. Roy S. Bryce-Laporte, pp. 321–28. New Brunswick, N.J.: Transaction Books.

De Vos, George, and Lola Romanucci-Ross, eds. 1975. *Ethnic Identity: Cultural Constituities and Change*. Palo Alto, Calif.: Mayfield.

Diaz, Alberto Pedro. 1973. Guanamaca: Une Communauté haïtienne à Cuba. *Sel* 9:28–37.

Diederich, Bernard, and Al Burt. 1964. *Papa Doc: The Truth about Haiti*. New York: McGraw-Hill.

Dominguez, Virginia R. 1975. *From Neighbor to Stranger: The Dilemma of*

Caribbean Peoples in the United States. New Haven: Antilles Research Program, Yale University.

Dominique, Gladys. 1965. *Table de composition d'aliments pour Haiti*. Port-au-Prince: Bureau de Nutrition, Département de la Santé Publique et de la Population.

Dorsinville, Roger. 1973. Les Haïtiens en Afrique. *Sel* 10:8–13.

Dow, Thomas. 1965. Primitive Medicine in Haiti. *Bulletin of the History of Medicine* 39:34–52.

Drake, St. Clair, and Horace R. Cayton. 1970. *Black Metropolis: A Study of Negro Life in a Northern City*. New York: Harcourt, Brace & World.

Du Bois, W. E. B. 1968. *The Autobiography of W. E. B. Du Bois: A Soliloquy on Viewing My Life from the Last Decade of Its First Century*. New York: International Publishers.

Duvalier, François. 1968. *Oeuvres essentielles: Eléments d'une doctrine*. Port-au-Prince: Imprimerie de l'Etat.

1969. *Mémoires d'un leader du tiers-monde*. Paris: Hachette.

Ehrlich, Richard L., ed. 1977. *Immigrants in Industrial America, 1850–1920*. Charlottesville: University Press of Virginia.

Elwell, Patricia, et al. 1977. Haitian and Dominican Undocumented Aliens in New York City: A Preliminary Report. *Migration Today* 5(5):5–9.

Epstein, A. L. 1978. *Ethos and Identity*. London: Tavistock.

Fass, Simon M. 1978. Families in Port-au-Prince: A Study of the Economics of Survival. Ph.D. dissertation, University of California, Los Angeles.

Fitzpatrick, Joseph P. 1971. *Puerto Rican Americans: The Meaning of Migration to the Mainland*. Englewood Cliffs, N.J.: Prentice-Hall.

Foner, Nancy. 1978. *Jamaica Farewell: Jamaican Migrants in London*. Berkeley: University of California Press.

1979. West Indians in New York City and London: A Comparative Analysis. *International Migration Review* 13(46):284–97.

Fontaine, Pierre Michel. 1976. Haitian Immigrants in Boston: A Commentary. In *Caribbean Immigration to the United States*, ed. Roy S. Bryce-Laporte and Delores M. Mortimer, pp. 111–29. Washington, D.C.: Research Institute on Immigration and Ethnic Studies, Smithsonian Institution.

Ford, Alice. 1964. *John James Audubon*. Norman: University of Oklahoma Press.

Fortes, Meyer. 1958. "Introduction." In *The Developmental Cycle in Domestic Groups*, ed. Jack Goody. Cambridge: Cambridge University Press.

Frazier, E. Franklin. 1939. The Negro Family in the United States. Chicago: University of Chicago Press.

Freidson, Eliot. 1966. Client Control and Medical Practice. In *Medical Care: Readings in the Sociology of Medical Institutions*, ed. W. Richard Scott and Edmund H. Volkart, pp. 259–71. New York: John Wiley.

Frucht, Richard. 1968. Emigration, Remittances, and Social Change: Aspects of the Social Field in Nevis, West Indies. *Anthropologica* 10(2):193–208.

Fuchs, Lawrence H. 1968. *American Ethnic Politics*. New York: Harper & Row.

Furnivall, J. S. 1948. *Colonial Policy and Practice: A Comparative Study of Burma and Netherlands India*. Cambridge: Cambridge University Press.

Gans, Herbert J. 1979. Symbolic Ethnicity: The Future of Ethnic Groups and Cultures in America. *Ethnic and Racial Studies* 2(1):1–20.

Garrison, Vivian. 1977. Doctor, Espírita, or Psychiatrist: Health-Seeking Behavior in a Puerto Rican Neighborhood of New York City. *Medical Anthropology* 1(2):65–180.

Garrison, Vivian, and Carol I. Weiss. 1979. Dominican Family Networks and United States Immigration Policy: A Case Study. *International Migration Review* 13(2):264–83.

Geertz, Clifford. 1962. The Rotating Credit Association: A "Middle Rung" in Development. *Economic Development and Cultural Change* 10(3):241–63.

Glazer, Nathan, and Daniel P. Moynihan. 1970. *Beyond the Melting Pot: The Negroes, Puerto Ricans, Jews, Italians, and Irish of New York City*. Cambridge: MIT Press.

Glazer, Nathan, and Daniel P. Moynihan, eds. 1975. *Ethnicity: Theory and Experience*. Cambridge: Harvard University Press.

Glick, Nina B. 1975. The Formation of a Haitian Ethnic Group. Ph.D. dissertation, Columbia University.

Gluckman, Max, ed. 1962. *Essays on the Ritual of Social Relations*. Manchester: Manchester University Press.

Goffman, Erving. 1961. *Asylums*. New York: Doubleday.

1967. *Interaction Ritual: Essays on Face-to-Face Behavior*. Chicago: Aldine.

1972. *Strategic Interaction*. Philadelphia: University of Pennsylvania Press.

Golab, Caroline. 1977. The Impact of the Industrial Experience on the Immigrant Family: The Huddled Masses Reconsidered. In *Immigrants in Industrial America,* ed. Richard L. Ehrlich, pp. 1–32. Charlottesville: University Press of Virginia.

Gollobin, Ira. 1979. Haitian "Boat People" and Equal Justice under Law: Background and Perspective. *Migration Today* 7(4):40–41.

Gonzalez, Nancie Solien. 1971. Peasant's Progress: Dominicans in New York. *Caribbean Studies* 10(3):154–71.

1976. Multiple Migratory Experiences of Dominican Women. *Anthropological Quarterly* 49:36–44.

Goody, Jack, ed. 1958. *The Developmental Cycle in Domestic Groups*. Cambridge: Cambridge University Press.

Gordon, Milton. 1964. *Assimilation in American Life*. New York: Oxford University Press.

Graham, Shirley. 1953. *Jean Baptiste Point Du Sable: Founder of Chicago*. New York: Julien Messner.

Graves, B. Nancy, and Theodore Graves. 1974. Adaptive Strategies in Urban Migration. In *Annual Review of Anthropology,* ed. Bernard J. Siegel, Alan R. Beals, and Stephen A. Tyler, vol. 3. Palo Alto, Calif.: Annual Reviews.

Greeley, Andrew M. 1976. Why Study Ethnicity? In *The Diverse Society*, ed. Pastora San Juan Caffertz and Leon Chestang, pp. 3–12. Washington, D.C.: National Association of Social Workers.

Greenfield, Sidney. 1961. Industrialization and the Family in Sociological Theory. *American Journal of Sociology* 68:312–22.

1966. *English Rustics in Black Skin: A Study of Modern Family Forms in a Pre-Industrialized Society*. New Haven: College and University Press.

Groom, Dale. 1961. Population Studies of Atherosclerosis. *Annals of Internal Medicine* 55:51–62.

Groom, Dale, et al. 1959. Coronary and Aortic Atherosclerosis in the Negroes of Haiti and the United States. *Annals of Internal Medicine* 51: 270–89.

1964. Haitian, American Negroes Reveal Differences in Coronary Disease at Adolescence. *Journal of the American Medical Association* 188:32–33.

Gross, Daniel R., and Barbara A. Underwood. 1971. Technological Change and Caloric Costs: Sisal Agriculture in Northeastern Brazil. *American Anthropologist* 73(3):725–40.

Grossman, Leona. 1976. Ethnicity and Health Delivery Systems. In *The Diverse Society*, ed. Pastora San Juan Caffertz and Leon Chestang, pp. 129–48. Washington, D.C.: National Association of Social Workers.

Gutman, Herbert G. 1976. *The Black Family in Slavery and Freedom*. New York: Pantheon.

Hacker, Andrew. 1975. *The New Yorkers: A Profile of an American Metropolis*. New York: Mason-Charter.

Handelman, Don. 1977. The Organization of Ethnicity. *Ethnic Groups* 1(3):187–200.

Handlin, Oscar. 1951. *The Uprooted: The Epic Story of the Great Migrations That Made the American People*. Boston: Little, Brown.

1959. *The Newcomers: Negroes and Puerto Ricans in a Changing Metropolis*. Garden City, N.Y.: Doubleday.

Hannerz, Ulf. 1974. Ethnicity and Opportunity in Urban America. In *Urban Ethnicity*, ed. Abner Cohen, pp. 37–76. London: Tavistock.

Hareven, Tamara K. 1977. Family and Work Patterns of Immigrant Laborers in a Planned Industrial Town, 1900–1930. In *Immigrants in Industrial America, 1850–1920*, ed. Richard L. Ehrlich, pp. 47–66. Charlottesville: University Press of Virginia.

Hartridge, Walter C. 1943. The Refugees from the Island of Saint Domingo in Maryland. *Maryland Historical Magazine* 38:103–22.

1944. The St. Dominguan Refugees in New Jersey. *New Jersey Historical Society Proceedings* 62(4):197–206.

Harwood, Alan. 1977. *Rx: Spirit as Needed: A Study of a Puerto Rican Community Mental Health Resource*. New York: John Wiley.

Harwood, Alan, ed. 1981. *Ethnicity and Medical Care*. Cambridge: Harvard University Press.

Hendricks, Glenn. 1974. *The Dominican Diaspora: From the Dominican Republic to New York City*. New York: Teachers College Press.

Herskovits, Melville, and Frances Herskovits. 1947. *Trinidad Village*. New York: Octagon Books.

Holly, James Theodore, and J. Dennis Harris. 1970. *Black Separatism and the Caribbean, 1860*. Ann Arbor: University of Michigan Press.

Holmes, Colin, ed. 1978. *Immigrants and Minorities in British Society*. London: George Allen & Unwin.

Hunt, Alfred Nathaniel. 1975. The Influence of Haiti on the Antebellum South, 1791–1865. Ph.D. dissertation, University of Texas, Austin.

Hunt, Benjamin S. 1860. *Remarks on Hayti as a Place of Settlement for Afric-Americans*. Philadelphia.

Hyndman, Albert. 1960. The West Indian in London. In *The West Indian Comes to England*, ed. S. K. Ruck. London: Routledge & Kegan Paul.

Ianni, Francis A. J. 1974. *Black Mafia: Ethnic Succession in Organized Crime*. New York: Simon & Schuster.

Institut Haïtien de Statistique. 1976. *Guide économique de la République d'Haiti*. Port-au-Prince: Département des Finances et des Affaires Economiques.

Jackson, J. A., ed. 1969. *Migration*. Cambridge: Cambridge University Press.

Jackson, Jacqueline Johnson. 1981. Urban Black Americans. In *Ethnicity and Medical Care*, ed. Alan Harwood. Cambridge: Harvard University Press.

Jadotte, Hérard. 1977. Haitian Immigration to Quebec. *Journal of Black Studies* 7:485–500.

Jelliffe, Derrick B., and E. F. Patricia Jelliffe. 1960. Prevalence of Protein-Calorie Malnutrition in Haitian Preschool Children. *American Journal of Public Health* 50:1355–66.

1961. The Nutritional Status of Haitian Children. *Acta Tropica* 18:1–45.

Jumelle, Julien. 1973. L'Opposition politique dans l'émigration haïtienne. *Sel* 10:38–51.

Justus, Joyce Bennett. 1976. West Indians in Los Angeles: Community and Identity. In *Caribbean Immigration to the United States*, ed. Roy S. Bryce-Laporte and Delores M. Mortimer, pp. 130–48. Washington, D.C.: Research Institute on Immigration and Ethnic Studies, Smithsonian Institution.

Kantrowitz, Nathan. 1973. *Ethnic and Racial Segregation in the New York Metropolis: Residential Patterns among White Ethnic Groups, Blacks, and Puerto Ricans*. New York: Praeger.

1976. New York Segregation: Implications for Social Policy. In *The Diverse Society*, ed. Pastora San Juan Caffertz and Leon Chestang, pp. 27–40. Washington, D.C.: National Association of Social Workers.

Kapferer, Bruce. 1969. Norms and the Manipulation of Relationships in a Work Context. In *Social Networks in Urban Situations*. Manchester: Manchester University Press.

Katzin, Margareth Fisher. 1959. Partners: An Informal Savings Institution in Jamaica. *Social and Economic Studies* 8(4):436–40.

Kerner Commission. 1972. Comparing the Immigrant and Negro Experience. In *Nation of Nations*, ed. Peter Rose, pp. 227–31. New York: Random House.

Kiev, Ari. 1961. Folk Psychiatry in Haiti. *Journal of Nervous and Mental Diseases* 132:260–65.

1962. Psychotherapy in Haitian Voodoo. *American Journal of Psychotherapy* 16:469–76.

King, James Lawrence. 1980. Haitian Refugee Center et al. (Plaintiffs) vs. Benjamin Civiletti et al. (Defendants): Final Order Granting Relief. July 2. Mimeo.

King, Kendall W. 1964. Development of All-Plant Food Mixture Using Crops Indigenous to Haiti: Amino-Acid Composition and Protein Quality. *Economic Botany* 18:311–22.

1967. *These Children Do Not Have to Die*. Port-au-Prince: Bureau de Nutrition, Département de la Santé Publique et de la Population.

1975. Nutrition Research in Haiti. In *The Haitian Potential: Research and Resources of Haiti*, ed. Vera Rubin and Richard P. Schaedel, pp. 147–56. New York: Teachers College Press.

King, Kendall W., Jean Foucauld, William Fougère, and Elmer L. Severinghaus. 1963a. Height and Weight of Haitian Children. *American Journal of Clinical Nutrition* 13:106–9.

King, Kendall W., W. H. Sebrell, Jr., Elmer L. Severinghaus, and Waldemar O. Snorvick. 1963b. Lysine Fortification of Wheat Bread Fed to Haitian School Children. *American Journal of Clinical Nutrition* 12:36–48.

King, Kendall W., William Fougère, and Ivan D. Béghin. 1966a. Un Mélange de proteines-végétales (AI-1000) pour les enfants haïtiens. *Annales de la Société Belge de Médecine Tropicale* 46:741–54.

King, Kendall W., William Fougère, Jean Foucauld, Gladys Dominique, and Ivan D. Béghin. 1966b. Response of Preschool Children to High Intakes of Haitian Cereal-Bean Mixtures. *Archivos Latino-Americanos de Nutrición* 16:53–64.

King, Kendall W., and Nelson O. Price. 1966a. Nutritional Value of Haitian Forages. *Archivos Latino-Americanos de Nutrición* 16:221–26.

1966b. Mineral Composition of Cereals and Legumes Indigenous to Haiti. *Archivos Latino-Americanos de Nutrición* 16:213–19.

King, Kendall W., Ivan D. Beghin, William Fougère, Gladys Dominique, R. Grinker, and Jean Foucauld. 1968a. Two Year Evaluation of a Nutritional Rehabilitation (Mothercraft) Center. *Archivos Latino-Americanos de Nutrición* 18:245–61.

King, Kendall W., Gladys Dominique, G. Uriodain, William Fougère, and Ivan D. Beghin. 1968b. Food Patterns from Dietary Surveys in Rural Haiti. *Journal of the American Dietetic Association* 53:114–18.

Klipstein, Frederick A., and Michael I. Samloff. 1966. Folate Synthesis by Intestinal Bacteria. *American Journal of Clinical Nutrition* 19:237–46.

Klipstein, Frederick A., Michael I. Samloff, and Eric A. Schenk. 1966. Tropical Sprue in Haiti. *Annals of Internal Medicine* 64:575–94.

Kristol, Irving. 1972. The Negro Today Is Like the Immigrant of Yesterday.

In *Nation of Nations*, Peter I. Rose, pp. 197–210. New York: Random House.

Kundstadter, Peter. 1963. A Survey of the Consanguine or Matrifocal Family. *American Anthropologist* 65:56–66.

Laguerre, Michel S. 1970. Brassages ethniques et émergence de la culture haïtienne. *Laurentian University Review* 3:48–65.

1976. *Migrations et vie rurale en Haïti*. Port-au-Prince: Institut Inter-Americain des Sciences Agricoles, Organisation des Etats Américains.

1978a. The Impact of Migration on Haitian Family and Household Organization. In *Family and Kinship in Middle America and the Caribbean*, ed. René Römer and Arnaud Marks, pp. 446–81. Leiden: Department of Caribbean Studies, Royal Institute of Linguistics and Anthropology; Cur açao: University of the Netherlands Antilles.

1978b. *Le Sangue haïtien: Un Système de crédit rotatoire*. Port-au-Prince: Inter-American Institute of Agricultural Sciences, Organization of American States.

1978c. Ticouloute and His Kinfolk: The Study of a Haitian Extended Family. In *The Extended Family in Black Societies*, ed. Demitri B. Shimkin et al., pp. 407–45. The Hague: Mouton.

1979a. The Haitian Niche in New York City. *Migration Today* 7:12–18.

1979b. *Etudes sur le Vodou haïtien*. Travaux du Centre de Recherches Caraïbes. Montreal: Presses de l'Université de Montréal.

1979c. *Schooling in Haiti*. Urban Diversity Series, no. 60. Eric Clearinghouse on Urban Education. New York: Teachers College, Columbia University.

1979d. Internal Dependency: The Structural Position of the Black Ghetto in American Society. *Journal of Ethnic Studies* 6(4):29–44.

1980a. Haitians in the United States. In *Harvard Encyclopedia of American Ethnic Groups*, ed. Stephan Thernstrom, Ann Orlov, and Oscar Handlin, pp. 446–49. Cambridge: Harvard University Press.

1980b. *Voodoo Heritage*. Foreword by Vera Rubin. Sage Library of Social Research, vol. 98. Beverly Hills, Calif.: Sage.

1981. Haitian-Americans. In *Ethnicity and Medical Care*, ed. Alan Harwood, pp. 172–210. Cambridge: Harvard University Press.

1982a. *Urban Life in the Caribbean*. Foreword by Richard Morse. Cambridge, Mass.: Schenkman.

1982b. *The Complete Haitiana: A Bibliographic Guide to the Scholarly Literature, 1900–1980*. 2 vols. Millwood, N.Y.: Kraus International Publications.

1983a. Haitian Immigrants in the United States: A Historical Overview. In *White Collar Migrants in the Americas and the Caribbean*, ed. Arnaud F. Marks and Hebe M. C. Vessuri, pp. 119–69. Leiden: Royal Institute of Linguistics and Anthropology.

1983b. The Haitian Political System. In *The Encyclopedia of Political Systems and Parties of the World*, ed. George G. Delury. New York: Facts-on-File.

n.d. Haitians in the Southern States. In *Encyclopedia of Southern Culture*, ed. William Ferris and Charles Wilson. Chapel Hill: University of North Carolina Press.

Laraque, Paul. n.d. Sur le sable de l'exil: Textes politiques. Unpublished manuscript.

Laurent, Gérard M. 1976. *Haïti et l'indépendance américaine*. Port-au-Prince: Séminaire Adventiste.

Laven, G. T. 1977. Diagnosis of Tuberculosis in Children Using Fluorescence Microscopic Examination of Gastric Washings. *American Review of Respiratory Disease* 115(5):743–49.

Ledur, Jean. 1973. L'Action politique des communautés haïtiennes à l'extérieur: Regards sur New York. *Bulletin du Front Haïtien d'Information et de Résistance* 5:9–10.

Lee, Hannah Farnham Sawyer. 1854. *Memoir of Pierre Toussaint, Born a Slave in St. Domingo*. Boston: Crosby, Nichols.

Lieberson, Stanley. 1963. *Ethnic Patterns in American Cities*. New York: Free Press.

Light, Ivan H. 1972. *Ethnic Enterprise in America: Business and Welfare among Chinese, Japanese, and Blacks*. Berkeley: University of California Press.

Little, Kenneth. 1965. *West African Urbanization: A Study of Voluntary Associations in Social Change*. Cambridge: Cambridge University Press.

Logan, R. W. 1941. *The Diplomatic Relations of the United States with Haiti, 1776–1891*. Chapel Hill: University of North Carolina Press.

Lyman, Stanford M., and William A. Douglass. 1973. Ethnicity: Strategies of Collective and Individual Impressions Management. *Social Research* 40: 344–65.

McCall, George J. 1963. Symbiosis: The Case of Hoodoo and the Numbers Racket. *Social Problems* 10(4):361–71.

McConnell, Roland C. 1968. *Negro Troops of Antebellum Louisiana: A History of the Battalion of Free Men of Color*. Baton Rouge: Louisiana State University Press.

McCready, William C. 1974. The Persistence of Ethnic Variation in American Families. In *Ethnicity in the United States: A Preliminary Reconnaissance*, ed. Andrew W. Greeley, pp. 156–76. New York: John Wiley.

1976. Social Utilities in a Pluralistic Society. In *The Diverse Society*, ed. Pastora San Juan Caffertz and Leon Chestang, pp. 13–25. Washington, D.C.: National Association of Social Workers.

MacDonald, John S., and Leatrice D. MacDonald. 1964. Chain Migration, Ethnic Neighborhood, and Social Networks. *Milbank Memorial Fund Quarterly* 42:82–97.

MacKenzie, Charles. 1830. *Notes on Haiti Made during Residence in the Republic*. Vol. 2. London: Henry Colburn & Richard Bentley.

McKinlay, J. B. 1972. Some Approaches and Problems in the Study of the Use of Services: An Overview. *Journal of Health and Social Behavior* 3 (April):115–51.

Mangin, W. 1967. Latin American Squatter Settlements: A Problem and a Solution. *Latin American Research Review* 2(3):65–98.

Manigat, Leslie. 1965. La Crise haïtiano-dominicaine de 1963–64. *Revue Française des Sciences Politiques* 15:288–96.

Manners, Robert A. 1965. Remittances and the Unit of Analysis in Anthropological Research. *Southwestern Journal of Anthropology* 21:179–95.

Marcelin, Milo. 1954. Cent Croyances et superstitions. *Optique* 7:48–56.

Marshall, Dawn I. 1979. *The Haitian Problem: Illegal Migration to the Bahamas*. Mona, Jamaica: Institute of Social and Economic Research, University of the West Indies.

Marshall, Roy E. 1974. A Study of Community Attitudes of Forty Haitians Living within the Brooklyn New York Community of Crown Heights. M.S.W. thesis, Hunter College, City University of New York.

Martin, Tony. 1976. *Race First: The Ideological and Organizational Struggles of Marcus Garvey and the Universal Negro Improvement Association*. Westport, Conn.: Greenwood Press.

Mathewson, Marie A. 1975. Is Crazy Anglo Crazy Haitian? *Psychiatric Annals* 5(8):79–83.

Mayers, Michael. 1982. Haitian Refugee Chronology and Update. *Refugees and Human Rights Newsletter*, Summer, pp. 11–12.

Mayfield, Julian. 1956. *The Hit*. New York: Vanguard Press.

Métraux, Alfred. 1953. Médecine et vodou en Haïti. *Acta Tropica* 10:28–68.

Meyers, Samuel, et al. 1977. Anemia and Intestinal Disfunction in Former Residents of the Caribbean. *Archives of Internal Medicine* 137:181–86.

Mims, Stewart L. 1947. Introduction to *American Journey*, by Moreau de Saint Méry, pp. ix-xxi. New York: Doubleday.

Mindel, Charles H., and Robert W. Habenstein. 1976. Family Life Styles of America's Ethnic Minorities: An Introduction. In *Ethnic Families in America: Patterns and Variations*, ed. Charles H. Mindel and Robert W. Habenstein, pp. 1–12. New York: Elsevier.

Mintz, Sidney, and Eric Wolf. 1950. An Analysis of Ritual Co-parenthood. *Southwestern Journal of Anthropology* 6:341–68.

Mintz, Sidney, and William Davenport, eds. 1961. Caribbean Social Organization. *Social and Economic Studies* 10(4) (special issue).

Mitchell, J. Clyde, ed. 1969. *Social Networks in Urban Situations*. Manchester: Manchester University Press.

Montague, Ludwell Lee. 1956. *Haiti and the United States, 1714–1938*. New York: Russell & Russell.

Moreau de Saint-Méry, Médéric Louis Elie. 1947. *American Journey*. New York: Doubleday.

Morin, Françoise. 1974. La femme haïtienne en diaspora. In *La Femme de couleur en Amérique Latine*, ed. Roger Bastide, pp. 211–20. Paris: Anthropos.

Mullings, Leith. 1978. Ethnicity and Stratification in the Urban United States. *Annals of the New York Academy of Sciences* 318:10–22.

Noël, Pierre. 1975. Recent Research in Public Health in Haiti. In *The Hai-*

tian Potential: Research and Resources of Haiti, ed. Vera Rubin and Richard P. Schaedel, pp. 157–66. New York: Teachers College Press.

Norvell, Douglass G., and James S. Wehrly. 1969. A Rotating Credit Association in the Dominican Republic. *Caribbean Studies* 9(1):45–52.

Osofsky, Gilbert. 1966. *Harlem: The Making of a Ghetto*. New York: Harper & Row.

Ottley, Roi, and William J. Weatherby. 1967. *The Negro in New York: An Informal Social History, 1626–1940*. New York: Praeger.

Padilla, Elena. 1958. *Up from Puerto Rico*. New York: Columbia University Press.

Palmer, Ransford W. 1976. Migration from the Caribbean to the States: The Economic Status of the Immigrants. In *Caribbean Immigration to the United States*, ed. Roy S. Bryce-Laporte, pp. 44–54. Washington, D.C.: Smithsonian Institution.

Patterson, Orlando. 1975. Context and Choice in Ethnic Allegiance: A Theoretical Framework and Caribbean Case Study. In *Ethnicity: Theory and Experience*, ed. Nathan Glazer and Daniel P. Moynihan, pp. 305–49. Cambridge: Harvard University Press.

1977. *Ethnic Chauvinism: The Reactionary Impulse*. New York: Stein & Day.

Philippe, Jeanne, and Jean Baptiste Romain. 1979. Indisposition in Haiti. *Social Science and Medicine* 13B(2):129–33.

Philpott, Stuart B. 1968. Remittance Obligations, Social Networks, and Choice among Montserratian Migrants in Britain. *Man* 6:465–76.

1973. *West Indian Migration*. London: Athlone Press.

Piè, Rolan. 1975. Kouman yo lévé ayisyin nouyok (Haitian children in New York). 23–24:9–18.

Pierre-Noël, Arsène V. 1959. *Les Plantes et les légumes d'Haïti qui guérissent: Mille et une recettes pratiques*. Port-au-Prince: Imprimerie de l'Etat.

Piore, Michael J. 1979. *Birds of Passage: Migrant Labor and Industrial Societies*. Cambridge: Cambridge University Press.

Pitchenik, Arthur, et al. 1982. The Prevalence of Tuberculosis and Drug Resistance among Haitians. *New England Journal of Medicine* 307 (July 15):162–65.

Portes, Alejandro, and Robert L. Bach. 1980. Immigrant Earnings: Cuban and Mexican Immigrants in the United States. *International Migration Review* 14(3):315–41.

Poux, Paddy. 1973. Haitians' Assimilation in the Life and the Future of the City of New York. M.S.W. thesis, Fordham University.

Preston, Julia, et al. 1979. Immigrant Workers in New York City. *NACLA Report on the Americas* 12(6):1–46.

Quarles, Benjamin. 1961. *The Negro in the American Revolution*. Chapel Hill: University of North Carolina Press.

Raphael, Lennox. 1964. West Indians and Afro-Americans. *Freedomways*, Summer, pp. 438–45.

Rawson, Ian G., and Gretchen G. Berggren. 1973. Family Structure, Child

Location, and Nutritional Disease in Rural Haiti. *Journal of Tropical Pediatrics* 19:288–98.

Reid, Ira de A. 1939. *The Negro Immigrant: His Background, Characteristics, and Social Adjustment, 1899–1937*. New York: Columbia University Press.

Rex, John. 1973. *Race, Colonialism, and the City*. London: Routledge & Kegan Paul.

Rey, Ketty H. 1970. *The Haitian Family: Implications for the Sex Education of Haitian Children in the United States*. New York: Community Service Society of New York, Department of Public Affairs.

Rosenwaike, Ira. 1972. *Population History of New York City*. Syracuse: Syracuse University Press.

Roucek, Joseph, and Francis J. Brown. 1939. The Problem of Negro and European Immigrant Minorities. *Journal of Negro Education* 3:299–312.

Rubin, Morton. 1960. Migration Patterns of Negroes from a Rural Northeastern Mississippi Community. *Social Forces* 39:59–66.

Ryan, Michael C. 1982. Political Asylum for the Haitians? *Case Western Reserve Journal of International Law* 14 (Winter):155–76.

Saintil, Michel. 1966. La Signification du cas Duvalier. *Frères du Monde* 43–44:89–104.

Samora, Julian, Lyle Saunders, and R. F. Larson. 1966. Medical Vocabulary Knowledge among Hospital Patients. In *Medical Care: Readings in the Sociology of Institutions*, ed. W. Richard Scott and Edmund H. Volkart, pp. 292–302. New York: John Wiley.

Sansaricq, Guy. 1978. Pastoral Guidelines for the Haitian Apostolate in the Diocese of Brooklyn. Queens, N.Y.: Haitian Apostolate Office.

1979. The Haitian Apostolate in Brooklyn. *Migration Today* 7(1):22–25.

Scarpa, Antonio. 1973. Appunti di etnoiatria haitiana (Notes on Haitian ethnomedicine). *Episteme* 7(4):298–303.

Scheiner, Seth. 1965. *Negro Mecca: A History of the Negro in New York City, 1865–1920*. New York: New York University Press.

Schey, Peter A. 1981. Haitian Refugee Center et al. (Plaintiffs-Appellees) v. Benjamin Civiletti et al. (Defendants-Appellants). On Appeal from the United States District Court for the Southern District of Florida. Brief for Appellees.

Schiller, Nina Glick. 1977. Ethnic Groups Are Made, Not Born: The Haitian Immigrants and American Politics. In *Ethnic Encounters: Identities and Contexts*, ed. G. L. Hicks and Philip Leis, pp. 23–37. Belmont, Calif.: Duxbury Press.

Schomburg, Arthur R. 1921. Military Services Rendered by the Haitians in the North and South American Wars for Independence. *A.M.E. Review* 37(4):199–212.

Scott, Clarissa S. 1974. Health and Healing Practices among Five Ethnic Groups in Miami, Florida. *Public Health Reports* 89:524–32.

1975. The Relationship between Beliefs about the Menstrual Cycle and Choice of Fertility Regulating Methods within 5 Ethnic Groups. *International Journal of Gynaecology and Obstetrics* 13(3):105–9.

1978. The Theoretical Significance of a Sense of Well-being for the Delivery of Gynecological Health Care. In *The Anthropology of Health*, ed. Eleanor E. Bauwens. St. Louis: Mosby.

Sears, M. L. 1972. Keratomalacia in Haiti. In *Causes and Prevention of Blindness*, ed. I. C. Michaelson and E. R. Berman. New York: Academic Press.

Sebrell, W. H., et al. 1959. Appraisal of Nutrition in Haiti. *American Journal of Clinical Nutrition* 7:538–84.

Segal, Aaron. 1975. Haiti. In *Population Policies in the Caribbean*, ed. Aaron Segal, pp. 177–215. Lexington, Mass.: D. C. Heath.

Seligman, Linda. 1977. Haitians: A Neglected Minority. *Personnel and Guidance Journal* 55(7):409–11.

Sheehan, Arthur, and Elizabeth Sheehan. 1955. *Pierre Toussaint: A Citizen of Old New York*. New York: P. J. Kennedy.

Shimkin, Demitri B., et al. 1978. *The Extended Family in Black Societies*. The Hague: Mouton.

Simmons, William J. 1968. *Men of Mark: Eminent, Progressive, and Rising*. New York: Arno Press and New York Times.

Sirinit, Kosol, Abdel-Gawad M. Soliman, Ali T. Van Loo, and Kendall W. King. 1965. Nutritional Value of Haitian Cereal-Legume Blends. *Journal of Nutrition* 86:415–23.

Smith, M. Estellie. 1972. Folk Medicine among the Sicilian-Americans of Buffalo, New York. *Urban Anthropology* 1 (Spring):87–106.

1976. Networks and Migration Resettlement: Cherchez la Femme. *Anthropological Quarterly* 49(1):20–27.

Smith, M. G. 1965. *The Plural Society in the British West Indies*. Berkeley: University of California Press.

1971. *West Indian Family Structure*. Seattle: University of Washington Press.

Smith, R. T. 1953. American Credit Institutions of Yoruba Type. *Man* 53 (February):32.

1956. *The Negro Family in British Guiana*. London: Routledge & Kegan Paul.

Snow, Loudell. 1977. Popular Medicine in a Black Neighborhood. In *Ethnic Medicine in the Southwest*, ed. Edward H. Spicer. Tucson: University of Arizona Press.

Soboul, Jan. 1975. Timoun nan fanmi ayisyin (Children in Haitian families). *Sel* 23–24:19–21.

Soler, René. 1980. *Etude pédagogique de conscientisation socio-politique, selon la méthode de Paulo Freire, en milieu immigré haïtien*. 2 vols. Département des Sciences de l'Education, Université de Montréal.

Sommer, Alfred, et al. 1976. Xerophthalmia and Anterior Segment Blindness. *American Journal of Ophthalmology* 82:439–46.

Souffrant, Claude. 1974. Les Haïtiens aux Etats-Unis. *Population* 2:133–46.

Sowell, Thomas. 1975. *Race and Economics*. New York: David McKay.

Spear, Allan H. 1967. *Black Chicago*. Chicago: University of Chicago Press.

Spector, Rachel E. 1979. *Cultural Diversity in Health and Illness*. New York: Appleton-Century-Crofts.

Spellman, Eugene P. 1982. Haitian Refugee Center, Inc., et al. (Plaintiffs) v. William French Smith et al. (Defendants). Memorandum Opinion. Case No. 81-1260-CIV-EPS, June 18. Mimeo.

Spurling, John J. 1962. Social Relations between American Negroes and British West Indians in Long Island City. Ph.D. dissertation, New York University.

Stack, Carol. 1974. *All Our Kin: Strategies for Survival in a Black Community*. New York: Harper & Row.

Sterkx, H. E. 1972. *The Free Negro in Ante-Bellum Louisiana*. Rutherford, N.J.: Fairleigh Dickinson University Press.

Taeuber, Karl E., and Alma F. Taeuber. 1964. The Negro as an Immigrant Group: Recent Trends in Racial and Ethnic Segregation. *American Journal of Sociology* 69:374–82.

1965. *Negroes in Cities*. Chicago: Aldine.

Tallant, Robert. 1971. *Voodoo in New Orleans*. New York: Collier.

Thompson, Bill. 1972. Mangoes Don't Grow in Brooklyn. *Revista Inter-Americana* 1(2):84–90.

Tilly, Charles, and C. Harold Brown. 1967. On Uprooting, Kinship, and the Auspices of Migration. *International Journal of Comparative Sociology* 8(2):139–64.

USAID (U.S. Agency for International Development). 1980. *Haiti*. Country Development Strategy Statement, FY 1982–86. Washington, D.C.

U.S. Congress, House of Representatives. 1976. Committee on the Judiciary, Subcommittee on Immigration, Citizenship, and International Law. *Hearings on Haitian Emigration*. 94th Cong., 2d sess.

1980. Committee on the Judiciary. *Hearings on the Caribbean Refugee Crisis: Cubans and Haitians*. 96th Cong., 2d sess.

U.S. Congress, Senate. 1922. Select Committee on Haiti and Dominican Republic. *Inquiry into the Occupation of Haiti and Santo Domingo*. 67th Cong., 2d sess.

1975. Statements of Rev. Jack Cassidy, Leonard F. Chapman, and Ira Gollobin. Committee on Foreign Relations, Subcommittee on International Organizations. *Hearings on Human Rights in Haiti*. 94th Cong., 1st sess., November 18.

Verdet, Paule. 1976. Trying Times: Haitian Youth in an Inner City High School. *Social Problems* 23(2):228–33.

Vieira, Jeffrey, et al. 1983. Acquired Immune Deficiency in Haitians: Opportunistic Infections in Previously Healthy Haitian Immigrants. *New England Journal of Medicine* 308:125–29.

Vincent, Joan. 1974. The Structuring of Ethnicity. *Human Organization* 33:375–79.

1978. Political Anthropology: Manipulative Strategies. *Annual Review of Anthropology* 7:175–94.

Vincent, Theodore G. 1972. *Black Power and the Garvey Movement*. San Francisco: Ramparts Press.

Vlach, John. 1975. Sources of the Shotgun House: African and Caribbean Antecedents for Afro-American Architecture. Ph.D. dissertation, Indiana University.

1977. Shotgun Houses. *Natural History* 86(2):51–57.

Vrga, Djuro J. 1971. Adjustment vs. Assimilation: Immigrant Minority Groups and Intra-Ethnic Conflicts. In *Ethnic Groups in the City: Culture, Institutions, and Power*, pp. 39–56. Lexington, Mass.: Heath.

Walsh, Bryan O. 1979. Haitians in Miami. *Migration Today* 7(4):42–44.

Wampler, Atlee W. 1980. Haitian Refugee Center et al. (Plaintiffs-Appellees) v. Benjamin Civiletti et al. (Defendants-Appellants). On Appeal from the United States District Court for the Southern District of Florida. Brief for Appellants. Mimeo.

Washington, John E. 1942. *They Knew Lincoln*. New York: Dutton.

Watson, Hilbourne A. 1976. International Migration and the Political Economy of Underdevelopment: Aspects of the Commonwealth Caribbean Situation. In *Caribbean Immigration to the United States*, ed. Roy S. Bryce-Laporte and Delores M. Mortimer, pp. 16–42. Washington, D.C.: Smithsonian Institution.

Weidman, Hazel Hitson. 1976. The Constructive Potential of Alienation: A Transcultural Perspective. In *Alienation in Contemporary Society*, ed. Roy S. Bryce-Laporte and Claudwell S. Thomas, pp. 335–57. New York: Praeger.

1978. *Miami Health Ecology Project Report: A Statement on Ethnicity and Health*. Vol. 1. Department of Psychiatry, University of Miami School of Medicine. Mimeo.

Wesley, Charles H. 1919. Lincoln's Plan for Colonizing the Emancipated Negroes. *Journal of Negro History* 4:7–21.

West, Susan. 1983. One Step behind a Killer: Sorting through the Clues to an Urgent Medical Mystery: AIDS. *Science 83* (March):36–45.

Whitten, Norman E. 1975. Jungle Quechua Ethnicity: An Ecuadorian Case Study. In *Migration and Development: Implications for Ethnic Identity and Political Conflict*, ed. Helen I. Safa and Brian M. Du Toit, pp. 144–73. The Hague: Mouton.

Whitten, Norman E., and Dorothea S. Whitten. 1972. Social Strategies and Social Relationships. *Annual Reviews of Anthropology* 1:247–70.

Wiese, H. Jean C. 1971. The Interaction of Western and Indigenous Medicine in Haiti in Regard to Tuberculosis. Ph.D. dissertation, University of North Carolina, Chapel Hill.

1974. Tuberculosis in Rural Haiti. *Social Science and Medicine* 8:359–62.

1976. Maternal Nutrition and Traditional Food Behavior in Haiti. *Human Organization* 35:193–200.

Wingfield, Roland C. 1966. Haiti: A Case Study of an Underdeveloped Area. Ph.D. dissertation, Louisiana State University.

Wirth, Louis. 1972. The Problem of Minority Groups. In *The Ethnic Experience and the Racial Crisis*, ed. Peter I. Rose, pp. 136–58. New York: Random House.

Woldemikael, Teklemarian. 1980. Maintenance and Change of Status in a

Migrant Community: Haitians in Evanston, Illinois. Ph.D. dissertation, Northwestern University.

Wood, Peter. 1974. *Black Majority: Negroes in Colonial South Carolina from 1670 through the Stono Rebellion*. New York: Knopf.

Woodson, Carter G. 1919. *The Education of the Negro to 1861*. Washington, D.C.: Associated Publishers.

World Bank. 1979. *Haiti: Urban Sector Survey*. Washington, D.C.

Wortham, Jacob. 1980. The Black Boat People. *Black Enterprise* 10(9): 32–36.

Yette, Samuel. 1971. *The Choice: The Issue of Black Survival in America*. New York: Putnam.

Zborowski, Mark. 1952. Cultural Components of Response to Pain. *Journal of Social Issues* 8:16–30.

Zola, Irving K. 1963. Observations on Gambling in a Lower Class Setting. *Social Problems* 19(4):353–61.

1964. Illness Behavior of the Working Class. In *Blue Collar World*, ed. Arthur Shostak and William Gomberg. Englewood Cliffs, N.J.: Prentice-Hall.

Index

Library of Congress Cataloging in Publication Data

Laguerre, Michel S.
American odyssey.

Includes bibliographical references and index.
1. Haitian Americans—New York (N.Y.) 2. Haitians—New York (N.Y.)
3. New York (N.Y.)—Foreign population. I. Title.
F128.9.H27L34 1984 305.8'9697294'07471 83-21078
ISBN 0-8014-1685-X
ISBN 0-8014-9270-X (pbk.)